BEGIN AGAIN

Redefining
Your Path to
a Fulfilling
Future.

LYNN CHITSATSO

Nurture & Equip

LYNN CHITSATSO

Begin Again

REDEFINING YOUR PATH TO A FULFILLING FUTURE.

First published in Great Britain by Nurture & Equip

ISBN: 978-1-9164768-3-7

PREFACE

In the vast tapestry of human existence, we often find ourselves at crossroads, facing unforeseen challenges, heartaches, and moments of profound uncertainty. In these defining moments, we yearn for a fresh start, a chance to rewrite the narrative of our existence. "Begin Again" is a compass for those who seek to navigate these uncharted waters, a guiding light for those who dare to embark on the journey of self-discovery and transformation.

This book is a testament to the resilience of the human spirit, a collection of stories, insights, and wisdom gathered from the lives of individuals who, against all odds, chose to begin again. Whether it is the tale of a courageous entrepreneur who bounced back from failure, a survivor who found hope after the darkest of nights, or a seeker who embarked on a quest for purpose, these stories illustrate the indomitable power of the human will.

Through the pages of "Begin Again," you will embark on a profound exploration of the art of renewal. It is a reminder that every ending carries within it the seeds of a new beginning, waiting to sprout and flourish. It invites you to shed the weight of the past, embrace the possibilities of the present, and forge a path to a brighter future.

In these pages, you will encounter insights from everyday individuals who have embarked on their personal odysseys of transformation. You will find practical strategies for overcoming setbacks, managing change, and nurturing resilience. Above all, you will discover that beginning again is not just an option; it is an inherent part of the human experience—a chance to rewrite your story, to evolve, and to become the author of your own destiny.

As you delve into the stories within, remember that life's greatest adventures often begin at the end of your comfort zone. "Begin Again" is an invitation to embark on that adventure, embrace the unknown, and find the strength and wisdom to write the next chapter of your life with hope, purpose, and unyielding determination.

So, dear reader, as you turn the page and embark on this journey, remember that every ending is a new beginning waiting to unfold. Your story is still being written, and within these words, you may discover the inspiration and guidance you need to take that first courageous step toward your own new beginning.

Welcome to "Begin Again."

— Lynn Chitsatso

CONTENTS

INTRODUCTION

Dear Reader,

I must start by expressing my sincere appreciation for your decision to pick up this book. It is not by chance that we have crossed paths; I genuinely believe that everything happens for a reason. So here we are, embarking on a new journey together, ready to begin again.

Life can be unpredictable, and sometimes it deals us heavy blows. Perhaps you have recently experienced a great loss, whether it be the end of a job or business venture, the painful dissolution of a marriage, or the heart-wrenching loss of a loved one. Maybe you find yourself stuck, unable to move forward due to a minor setback or a string of unfortunate events. It is even possible that you have been betrayed or feel abandoned, left to pick up the pieces of your life on your own. Or, you may be facing a lifelong illness, desperately seeking guidance on how to carry on and find the strength to start anew.

The thought of beginning again can be daunting, and the fear of failure may consume you. But dear reader, I want you to ask yourself which path you would rather take, staying trapped in fear or summoning the courage to step boldly towards a life filled with fulfilment and success. I firmly believe that by adhering to The 10 R's of Beginning Again, you can reach the destination you desire.

As you journey through the pages of this book, my hope is that by the time you reach the last page, you will be able to write a heartfelt letter to yourself. A letter filled with self-love and acceptance, embracing every aspect of who you are, flaws and all. You are human, and that means making mistakes and experiencing moments of imperfection. But it is in these very moments that growth and resilience are nurtured.

I want you to look at yourself in the mirror and see the beauty that lies within. Embrace your scars, both physical and emotional, for they tell a story of the battles you have fought and the strength you possess. I admire your tenacity, your ability to pick yourself up when everything feels lost and lonely. I applaud the steps you have taken to change, even when it cost you dearly.

Though no one may truly understand the price you have paid for your healing, there is one who does – God. Healing is a painful process, and

I commend your unwavering commitment to see it through. You have endured judgment, abandonment, scorn, and the cruelty of others, but you have not allowed it to deter you. Your impact on this world is profound, and it is through your unshakeable spirit that you continue to make a difference.

I am fascinated by the fact that you look in the mirror and smile at what you see. You possess a beauty that radiates from within – from your beautiful eyes and cheeks to your radiant smile and flawless teeth. But your beauty is not limited to your physical appearance. Your soul is beautiful, bold, and compassionate. You emit an aura of love, generosity, and discernment. You possess wisdom and strength, and you refuse to be fooled easily.

You are gifted, amazing, and destined for greatness. You are not meant to hide in the shadows; instead, you are meant to shine bright as the sun. You exude righteousness, patience, and an unyielding spirit. You are the best person I have ever had the privilege of knowing. Your intelligence, wit, and company are cherished. You are strong yet tender, honest yet gentle.

Yes, vulnerability may have led you astray in the past, but that does not diminish its importance. Embracing vulnerability allows you to find freedom, the freedom to be your authentic self. Life is a journey, and you have shed countless tears along the way. But you have also experienced laughter and joy. I commend your intentionality in choosing self-care and prioritizing joy over sadness.

Gone are the days where pain dominates your life; you have declared that this is not your default setting. Instead, you embrace peace, joy, and righteousness. You attract goodness, mercy, fortune, healthy relationships, progress, and favour. The time has come, my dear reader, to begin again.

With warm regards,
Lynn Chitsatso

CHAPTER 1:

SOUL-SEARCHING: ENGAGING IN CANDID DIALOGUES WITH YOURSELF - SELF-REFLECTION

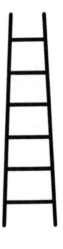

Behind schedule

Behind schedule is a term used when you have not met your targets or your goals. Or just behind in life. Sometimes it is due to lack of planning sometimes, circumstances show up along the way. Sometimes it is lack of knowledge, lack of insight or foresight. Whatever reason that it all comes back to being behind schedule. How do you move on from this? Before we get onto that, let us look at the consequences of being behind schedule.

When you are behind schedule in a work setting, it might cause a lot of problems; it might make the project lag, and you may end up losing your client and potential income because of that. Along the way, you might lose your confidence as a person. You may be stressed and question yourself, affecting your self-esteem, and may end up having mental health issues. Whatever the setting, it can lead to any of this depending on where you are as a person. Some people can handle disappointments and mishaps well. Their ability to bounce back is remarkable. Whereas some people struggle to move on.

Throughout our childhood, we all harboured dreams and aspirations for our future. We envisioned the kind of life we would have - the perfect home, the ideal partner, the prestigious career, and the luxurious car. However, life rarely goes according to plan, leaving many of us in our thirties, forties, fifties, or even older with unresolved questions and a lingering sense of disappointment.

As we compare our current situation to the dreams we once had, we may find ourselves disqualifying our worth, believing that we did not meet the predetermined timeline of success. We tell ourselves that by this stage of life, we should have children who are nearing university or building families of their own. But instead, we may be childless and single, feeling behind and uncertain about what the future holds. As we scrutinize our age and life choices, we question whether our dreams will ever come to fruition.

When we realize that we are behind schedule, the feeling can be overwhelming. Whether it is a mere year or a decade, the challenge of catching up becomes daunting. We consider all the factors that come into play - location, age, aspirations, and current circumstances - and wonder if it is even possible to bridge the gap. Our bodies may not be as resilient as before, our minds might not be as sharp, and our education level and income may not align with our dreams. Additionally, our relationships may have suffered setbacks or disappointments along the way. Life can be relentless in testing us, leaving us wondering where we went wrong and how we can make up for lost time.

In moments like these, tears may flow, and we may lament over the choices we made and what we could have done differently. But dwelling in the past only perpetuates disappointment and pain. Instead, we must gather the strength to recover and forge ahead. We must dare to dream again, not just trimming our aspirations to fit the time we have left but believing that the biggest dreams are still within reach. It is time to reassess the missing pieces of our lives and determine what truly matters.

So, where do we start? How do we pick up the pieces and rebuild our lives? The answer lies in engaging with the opportunities that come our way. We must evaluate what we are capable of and grab onto those opportunities with firm resolve. It may seem daunting, but we have no time to waste. We must not get caught up in doubt or distractions; instead, we must focus on our purpose and run towards it with unwavering determination.

In this journey of recovery, we might encounter resistance. The voices of doubt will shout the loudest, urging us to turn back, telling us that we are too old or incapable of achieving our dreams. Yet, amid the cacophony of negativity, there is one voice that matters the most - the voice within us. We must silence the doubts and insecurities within us and keep pushing forward. With every step, we must remind ourselves that we can do it, that we have what it takes to overcome any obstacles in our path.

This pursuit of a fulfilled life may not be easy, and recovery may come with its fair share of pain. However, we must embrace and accept the discomfort as part of the process. We must carefully choose the right path to pursue, seeking help when needed and staying focused on the ultimate goal. Without looking back or sideways, we must keep our gaze fixed on the future and relentlessly work towards making every day count.

So, let us not succumb to the pressures of time or the judgments of others. Instead, let us compete with ourselves, consistently striving to be better and reach higher. We must shut down the voices that tell us we cannot and replace them with a resounding belief that we can. Each day, as the voice of doubt whispers, we must quash it and keep grinding until we achieve our dreams. In this very moment, we declare that we can do it, and we will not stop until we prove it to ourselves and the world. Watch us as we rise and conquer the challenges that lie ahead.

Emily's story

Emily a young woman, lived in a small quiet town of Brook. She had always been a dreamer with big aspirations and a heart full of ambition.

But life had a funny way of playing tricks on her, and she found herself constantly behind schedule.

As she reached her thirties, Emily could not help but feel discouraged. She had imagined a different life for herself - a successful career, a loving family, and a beautiful home. Yet, here she was, still searching for her purpose and feeling behind in every aspect of her life. One gloomy evening, as Emily sat by her window, watching the rain pour outside, she felt a sudden urge to rewrite her story. She realized that dwelling on her past mistakes and missed opportunities would only hold her back. It was time to embrace her journey and make the most of the present.

With renewed determination, Emily began to dream again. She started by identifying what was missing in her life and setting goals to bridge the gap. She enrolled in courses to gain new skills, networked with like-minded individuals, and took on challenging projects to prove her capabilities.

But it was not all smooth sailing. Emily faced countless obstacles and setbacks along the way. There were times when she questioned her worth and wanted to give up. Yet, she refused to let her past dictate her future. With the support of her loved ones and a resilient spirit, she pressed on.

As the years went by, Emily saw her life transform. She built a successful career filled with purpose and fulfilment. She surrounded herself with a loving and supportive circle of friends and family. And most importantly, she found the courage to rewrite her own narrative, embracing her journey despite the delays.

Looking back, Emily realized that being behind schedule was not a setback but an opportunity for growth. It taught her resilience, perseverance, and the importance of self-belief. She understood that life does not always go according to plan, but the ability to adapt and rewrite our stories truly defines us.

So, if you ever find yourself feeling behind schedule, take a page from Emily's book. Embrace the unexpected twists and turns, dream big, and rewrite your story. Because in the end, it is not about when you reach your goals but the journey you take to get there. And who knows, you might just end up with a story more captivating than you ever imagined.

REFLECT

Your experiences:

Reflect on what has worked and what did not in your previous attempt? Consider the mistakes you made, the lessons you learned, and the skills you acquired.

WHY REFLECT?

In the vast tapestry of human existence, there exists a singular and profound phenomenon that holds immeasurable power: reflection. It is the art of introspection, the act of gazing inward to explore the depths of our souls. A captivating journey into oneself, reflection unravels the mysteries of our thoughts, emotions, and experiences. It is a sacred voyage that calls upon us to ponder the essence of our being and the path we tread upon. This captivating tale weaves through the myriad of reasons why we must reflect, illuminating the essence of this timeless practice.

To reflect is to pause amidst the ceaseless whirlwind of life, to find solace in the stillness of our thoughts. It is in these moments of contemplation that our truest selves emerge, shedding the mundane concerns of daily existence and embracing the profound wisdom that resides within us. As we delve into the complexities of our minds, we discover a world of possibilities, unearthing hidden desires and aspirations that lay dormant, waiting to be explored.

In the chaos of our modern lives, reflection offers respite, enabling us to gain clarity and perspective on the challenges we face. When we step back from the commotion and immerse ourselves in thoughtful introspection, the noise dissipates, allowing us to discern the subtle nuances that evaded our attention. In this serene haven, we find both answers and questions, for reflection is not a vessel solely of certainty but a catalyst for profound inquiry and growth.

Through reflection, we cultivate a heightened sense of self-awareness, acknowledging our strengths and weaknesses with a newfound clarity. It is within this realm of self-discovery that we learn to embrace our flaws, recognizing that they are the threads that weave the tapestry of our humanity. As we gaze upon our reflection, we stand face-to-face with the imperfect beings that we are, forging a path towards self-acceptance and resilience.

Furthermore, reflection is a potent tool for personal growth and development. As we pause to examine our past choices and experiences, we extract valuable lessons that guide our future endeavours. With an open mind and heart, we dissect the triumphs and tribulations, extracting wisdom from each misstep and victory alike. In this perpetual cycle of discovery, we unleash the full extent of our potential, nurturing the seeds of progress and evolution.

Beyond the individual, reflection has the power to unite communities and foster deeper connections amongst humanity. As we collectively reflect upon the world around us, we develop empathy, compassion, and a shared understanding. By peering into the depths of our souls, we confront our biases and preconceptions, fostering a profound sense of openness that enables meaningful dialogue and collaboration. It is through reflection that we embrace the diversity that enriches our existence, recognizing that our perspectives intertwine to create a tapestry that is greater than the sum of its parts.

In conclusion, reflection is a captivating journey into the recesses of our souls, a timeless practice that calls upon us to pause, ponder, and explore the depths within. Through introspection, we uncover our truest selves, gaining clarity and perspective in the chaos of our lives. It is within the realm of reflection that we nurture personal growth and development, unlocking the potential that resides within. Furthermore, it is through this introspective voyage that we forge connections, unite communities, and foster empathy amongst ourselves. As we embark upon this captivating practice, let us embrace the profound wisdom that lies in reflection, allowing it to illuminate our paths and guide us towards a brighter, more enlightened future.

May's Story

In a small, small town in Wales, nestled, surrounded by hills, there lived an aspiring writer named May. She had always dreamt of writing a book that would captivate readers' hearts and take them on a magical journey. However, her previous attempts at creating a compelling story had fallen short, leaving her disheartened and pondering over where she had gone wrong.

With a determined spirit and a strong desire to improve, May decided to embark on a journey of self-reflection. She dove into her past experiences, determined to understand what had worked and what had not. She delved deep into her memories, scouring through the lessons she had learned and the mistakes she had made.

As May reflected on her past attempts, the reasons behind her shortcomings started to surface. She realized that she lacked a clear vision and purpose for her stories. They had been mere fragments of her imagination, lacking the depth and substance that only a well-thought-out narrative could provide. She knew that to craft a compelling book, she needed to answer the whys and wherefores of her storytelling.

With newfound determination, May began to establish a solid foundation for her writing. She asked herself the vital question of why she wanted to author a compelling book. The answer resonated deep within her soul - she wanted to touch people's lives, evoke emotions, and create a lasting impact. Armed with this purpose, she set out to weave a tale that would resonate with readers on a profound level.

Next, May pondered upon the 'who.' Who were the characters that would bring her story to life? She realized that the key to captivating readers lay in creating relatable and multidimensional characters. She embarked on a journey to understand the depths of human emotions, studying psychology and exploring the intricacies of the human condition. With every piece of knowledge she acquired, her characters began to evolve, reflecting the intricacies and complexities of real people.

As she dug deeper into her past experiences, May also analysed the when and where of her stories. She understood that the setting and time were crucial elements in connecting readers to her narrative. She researched historical events, cultural nuances, and breathtaking locations, ensuring that her story would transcend mere words and transport readers to a different time and place altogether.

However, May knew that true storytelling was not just about answering the 'who,' why, and where. It was also about the how and the what. How would she engage readers from the very first page? How would she keep them hooked until the very end? And what plot twists and turns would she employ to surprise and delight her audience?

With each passing day, May dedicated herself to honing her writing skills. She read voraciously, studied the works of literary giants, and attended writing workshops to refine her craft. Armed with a newfound understanding of narrative structure and pacing, she began to mould her story with care and precision. Each sentence built upon the next, like the brushstrokes of an expert artist, creating a mesmerizing tapestry of words that would leave readers spellbound.

Finally, after months of dedicated effort, May completed her manuscript. As she penned the final sentence, she felt an overwhelming sense of achievement and fulfilment. She knew that she had poured her heart and soul into creating a compelling book that would touch the lives of readers worldwide.

Little did May know; her journey of reflection had not only transformed her as a writer but also as a person. Through introspection and self-accountability, she had not only honed her writing skills but had also discovered her own voice and purpose.

And so, armed with her captivating book in hand, May set forth on a new adventure, ready to share her enchanting tale with the world and to inspire others to embark on their own journeys of self-reflection and creative growth.

Here is another honest conversation Sarah had with herself.

The sun dipped below the horizon, casting a golden hue across the room as Sarah sat at her desk, ready to embark on a journey of reflection. It had been a long day, filled with challenges, doubts, and an overwhelming desire to move forward. She knew that to break free from her current state of feeling stuck, she needed to have an honest conversation with herself.

As Sarah closed her eyes and took a deep breath, memories flooded her mind like a fast-paced movie reel. She reflected on her past experiences, the successes, but most importantly, the failures. It was in these failures that she discovered her true strength and resilience.

She recalled the first time she tried to start a business. The excitement and enthusiasm radiated from her every pore, but as the days turned to weeks, and the weeks to months, she realized that success didn't come overnight. Sarah acknowledged the mistakes she made, but rather than allowing them to define her, she saw them as stepping stones to growth.

The lessons she learned were etched in her heart. She understood the importance of perseverance, patience, and the ability to adapt. Sarah had gained a newfound knowledge that would guide her in her future endeavours.

But it wasn't just about the mistakes; Sarah also recognized the skills she had acquired along the way. She had learned to network, to communicate effectively, and to think critically. These were not just abstract skills but the building blocks of success that she could rely on to pave a path forward.

As Sarah's thoughts started to wander, she began to question the purpose behind her desire to move ahead. Why did she want to break free from her current state? What was her goal? She realized that, deep down, she craved fulfilment, both personally and professionally.

Sarah knew that her breakthrough would come not just from external achievements but from the fulfilment she found within herself. It was in these honest moments of reflection that she discovered her true worth, her passions, and her purpose.

With clarity in mind, Sarah delved into another layer of introspection – the "who." Who was she accountable to? Who would be her support system on this journey? She understood that while the path might be winding and steep, she wouldn't have to face it alone.

Sarah identified her closest confidants – her unwavering best friend, her supportive family, and the mentor who had believed in her from day one. These were the individuals who would hold her accountable, cheer her on during victories, and lift her up during defeat.

As the moon rose high in the sky, casting a gentle glow through the window, Sarah shifted her focus to the "when" and the "which." When would she start acting? Which opportunities would she embrace? She knew that reflection was only the first step; action was what would lead her down the path of progress.

Filled with optimism, Sarah picked up her pen and wrote down her goals, aspirations, and actionable steps. With each stroke of the pen, she felt a surge of energy and determination. She knew that tomorrow; she would begin her journey towards a brighter future.

Reflecting on her past experiences, Sarah had discovered the power she held within. She understood that mistakes and failures were not hurdles but rather opportunities for growth. Through this honest conversation with herself, Sarah had unlocked her potential and found the inspiration to overcome the feeling of being stuck.

As Sarah closed her notebook and prepared for a restful night's sleep, she knew that the road ahead might not be easy. But armed with her reflections and the lessons she had learned; she was ready to face any challenge that came her way.

For Sarah, this chapter was not just a book but a turning point in her life. She had set the stage for a remarkable journey of self-discovery, growth, and triumph. With every word she had written, Sarah was ready to seize her destiny and create a life that surpassed her wildest dreams.

Evelyn's story,

Evelyn sat at her kitchen table, the morning sunlight streaming through the window, casting a warm glow on the room. As she sipped her coffee, her mind wandered to the various moments that had brought her to this point in her life. Lately, she had been feeling stuck, as if life was passing her by.

She reflected on her past experiences, and the ups and downs that had shaped her journey. There were times of immense joy and fulfilment, like when she held her newborn daughter in her arms for the first time. The love that welled up within her was indescribable, and she knew that becoming a mother was one of the most profound experiences she had ever had.

But there were also challenges along the way. The struggles of balancing motherhood and a career had often left her feeling overwhelmed and stretched thin. She had made sacrifices and compromises, putting her own dreams on hold to ensure the well-being of her family. While she cherished her role as a mother, there were times when she could not help but wonder what could have been if she had pursued her own passions more fervently.

As Evelyn delved deeper into her reflections, she realized that the key to feeling unstuck was not dwelling on missed opportunities or regretting the choices she had made. Instead, it was about finding a sense of gratitude for the path she had taken and the lessons she had learned along the way.

She thought about the strength and resilience she had developed through the challenges she had faced. Each obstacle taught her to be more adaptable, patient, and compassionate. Evelyn realized that these qualities were invaluable in navigating life's twists and turns.

With a renewed sense of purpose, Evelyn embraced the present moment and redefined her future. She began exploring new hobbies and reconnecting with old passions that she had set aside. She started painting again, finding solace and joy in the vibrant colours and creative expression. Evelyn also sought support from her loved ones and reached out to a community of like-minded individuals who shared her interests. Through these connections, she found inspiration, encouragement, and a sense of belonging.

As time passed, Evelyn discovered that life was not about reaching a destination but rather about the journey itself. It was about embracing the ebb and flow, the highs, and lows, and finding fulfilment in the everyday moments. She realized that even though she felt stuck, she had the power to shape her own path and create a future that aligned with her values and desires.

Armed with her newfound perspective, Evelyn embarked on a new chapter of her life. She cherished her role as a mother, continued to pursue her passions, and found contentment in the journey of self-discovery. The feeling of being stuck slowly faded away, replaced by a sense of purpose and fulfilment that radiated from within.

The steps Evelyn took to be fulfilled.

As Evelyn embarked on her journey of self-discovery, she began setting goals that would bring her a sense of fulfilment and purpose. These goals encompassed various aspects of her life, allowing her to explore different areas and find joy in each pursuit. Here are some of the goals Evelyn set:

Personal Growth: Evelyn prioritized her own personal growth and well-being. She set aside time each day for self-reflection and introspection. She practiced mindfulness and meditation, which helped her cultivate a sense of inner peace and clarity.

Pursuing Passions: Evelyn made it a goal to rediscover and pursue her passions. She reignited her love for painting and committed to dedicating regular time to engage in this creative outlet. She enrolled in art classes and workshops to improve her skills and expand her artistic horizons.

Career Development: While Evelyn had temporarily put her career on hold to focus on motherhood, she recognized the importance of professional fulfilment. She explored opportunities for professional development, such as attending seminars, taking online courses, and networking within her industry. She set a goal to take small steps towards reestablishing her career when the time felt right.

Health and Well-being: Taking care of her physical and mental health became a priority for Evelyn. She set goals related to regular exercise, such as joining a fitness class or incorporating daily walks into her routine. She also focused on nourishing her body with healthy foods and maintaining a balanced lifestyle.

Connecting with Others: Evelyn understood the value of human connection and sought to build meaningful relationships. She tried to connect with old friends and family members, arranging gatherings and outings. She also joined social groups and communities centred around her interests, providing her with a supportive network of like-minded individuals.

Giving Back: Evelyn felt a strong desire to give back to her community. She set a goal to volunteer her time and skills to organizations that aligned with her values. Whether it was mentoring young artists or contributing to a local charity, she found fulfilment in making a positive impact on the lives of others.

Embracing New Experiences: Evelyn vowed to step out of her comfort zone and embrace new experiences. She sought out opportunities to

travel, explore diverse cultures, and broaden her perspective. Trying new activities, visiting new places, and engaging in diverse experiences allowed her to expand her horizons and find inspiration in the world around her.

By setting goals, Evelyn created a roadmap for her journey towards fulfilment. Each goal represented a step forward, bringing her closer to a life that resonated with her values and aspirations. Through dedication, perseverance, and a newfound sense of purpose, she was able to fill her life with meaning and joy.

By following these steps, you can make the process of beginning again more manageable and increase your chances of success. Remember that everyone's journey is unique, and staying patient and compassionate with yourself is important as you navigate this transition.

Reflect

How do I walk away from that which has been holding me back

Walking away from something that has been holding you back can be a difficult and challenging process, but here are some steps that may help:

Identify what has been holding you back: The first step in walking away from something that has been holding you back is to identify what it is. This could be a person, a job, a habit, or a belief.

Consider the consequences of staying: Once you have identified what has been holding you back, consider the consequences of staying in that situation. Think about how it is affecting your life and what you are missing by not moving forward.

3. Set clear goals: Setting clear goals can help you focus on what you want to achieve and give you the motivation to move forward. Write down your goals and plan for how you will achieve them.

4. Seek support: Walking away from something that has been holding you back can be challenging, so it is important to seek support from 9 friends, family, or a counsellor. They can provide encouragement and help you stay on track.

5. Act: Once you have identified what has been holding you back, and have set clear goals and sought support, it's time to take action. This could mean ending a toxic relationship, quitting a job that is not fulfilling, breaking a bad habit, or challenging a limiting belief.

6. Stay committed: Walking away from something that has been holding you back requires commitment and perseverance. Stay focused on your goals and remind yourself of the reasons why you decided to make a change.

7. Celebrate your progress: Celebrate each step forward, no matter how small it may seem. Recognize your progress and take pride in your accomplishments.

Remember, walking away from something that has been holding you back is not easy, but it is worth it. It takes courage and determination to make a change, but by following these steps, you can move towards a more fulfilling and rewarding life.

- Take the time to look back on past experiences, both positive and negative, that have shaped who you are today. Consider how these experiences have contributed to the person you are now and what skills they have given you along the way.

CHAPTER 2:

PARDON AND REJUVENATE: GRANTING FORGIVENESS AND REFRESHING YOUR MIND

Repent- forgive yourself and anybody involved, Repent. Renew- your mind.

Letting Go of the Twins: Unforgiveness and Bitterness

Unforgiveness and bitterness are two powerful emotions that often hold us back from reaching our full potential. They act as formidable barriers, hindering personal growth and progress. Just like twins, they intertwine and feed off each other, injecting negativity, and toxicity into our lives. Addressing and eliminating these burdensome emotions are pivotal steps towards achieving happiness, peace, and success. This chapter will delve into the consequences of harbouring unforgiveness and bitterness, exploring strategies to overcome them and highlighting the transformative power of forgiveness.

Unforgiveness is a destructive force that can have severe consequences on an individual's emotional, mental, and even physical well-being. Holding onto resentment and refusing to forgive those who have wronged us keeps us anchored to the past, preventing us from moving forward. It takes up valuable mental and emotional space, draining our energy and creating constant hostility. As poet Marianne Williamson once said, "Unforgiveness is like drinking poison and hoping the other person dies."

Bitterness is a poison that consumes; the twin-like companion of unforgiveness, bitterness is equally detrimental. Bitterness arises from a prolonged state of resentment or disappointment, often fuelled by unforgiveness. It permeates every aspect of our lives, poisoning relationships, tainting our outlook, and robbing us of joy and contentment. It breeds a negative mindset and prevents us from experiencing true happiness. Furthermore, studies have shown that harbouring bitterness can adversely impact one's health, leading to increased stress levels, heart problems, and compromised immune functioning.

Mandela story

One real-life example of someone who transformed their life by letting go of unforgiveness and bitterness is Nelson Mandela. Mandela spent 27 years in prison during the apartheid era in South Africa. Despite facing immense injustice and cruelty, he chose to release the bitterness and resentment he could have held towards his oppressors.

Upon his release in 1990, Mandela became a prominent advocate for peace, reconciliation, and forgiveness. He played a key role in ending apartheid and worked towards fostering unity and reconciliation among different racial groups in the country. Mandela's ability to let go of bitterness and forgive his oppressors played a crucial role in his efforts to build a rainbow nation.

He actively promoted forgiveness and reconciliation through initiatives such as the Truth and Reconciliation Commission, which allowed victims and perpetrators to come forward and share their experiences to foster healing. Mandela's personal transformation from prisoner to president, along with his commitment to forgiveness and unity, remains an inspiring example of the power of letting go of unforgiveness and bitterness to bring about positive change at a societal level.

Overcoming Unforgiveness and Bitterness:

Breaking free from the clutches of unforgiveness and bitterness requires conscious effort and a willingness to let go. Here are some practical ways to guide individuals towards healing and progress:

1. Acknowledge and accept the pain: Recognition and acceptance of the pain caused by the actions of others are

crucial initial steps. Validating our emotions allows us to better understand the power these emotions hold over us.

2. Practice empathy and perspective-taking: Stepping into the shoes of those who have wronged us can foster empathy and understanding. This does not excuse their behaviour but helps us see them as flawed individuals, capable of both good and bad choices.

3. Cultivate forgiveness: Forgiveness is a choice and a process, not a single act. It involves letting go of resentment, relinquishing the desire for revenge, and choosing compassion instead. This can be achieved through therapy, self-reflection, or seeking support from loved ones.

4. Focus on self-care and growth: Prioritizing self-care and personal growth is essential to healing wounds and fostering resilience. Engaging in activities that bring joy, investing in hobbies, and seeking therapy or counselling can aid in rebuilding self-esteem and fostering forgiveness.

The act of repentance plays a crucial role in personal growth and self-reflection.

Repentance requires acknowledging and accepting responsibility for one's mistakes or wrongdoings. This process enables individuals to confront their own shortcomings and take ownership of their actions. It encourages them to be honest with themselves about their behaviour or decisions.

Repentance fosters a sense of humility as individuals must acknowledge that they are not perfect and have made errors. This humility allows individuals to open themselves up to learning, growth, and self-reflection. It helps in overcoming ego-driven behaviours and encourages a more introspective mindset.

Repentance involves reflecting on past actions and identifying the lessons to be learned. It allows individuals to understand the consequences of their actions and make a conscious effort not to repeat the same mistakes in the future. Through repentance, people gain insights into their values, priorities, and the impact they have on others.

Repentance often involves seeking forgiveness from those who may have been affected by one's actions. This process necessitates understanding and empathizing with the feelings and experiences of others. It encourages individuals to consider the impact of their behaviour on others, promoting the development of empathy, compassion, and a greater sense of interconnectedness.

Repentance is a proactive step towards personal growth and self-improvement. By acknowledging mistakes, taking responsibility, and seeking forgiveness, individuals demonstrate a willingness to learn and grow from their past actions. They actively engage in the process of self-reflection, setting themselves on a path of continuous self-improvement.

The act of repentance helps individuals focus on their core values, ethics, and principles. It provides an opportunity to align personal actions with these values, reinforcing one's character and commitment to personal growth. By reflecting on their mistakes and seeking forgiveness, individuals cultivate virtues like integrity, honesty, and accountability.

The act of repentance contributes to personal growth and self-reflection by fostering introspection, accountability, humility, empathy, and the continuous pursuit of self-improvement. It allows individuals to learn from their mistakes, develop resilience, and move forward with greater maturity and understanding.

Forgiveness is good for you for many reasons. It includes an improved mental health: Holding onto anger and resentment can be detrimental to your mental health, leading to increased stress, anxiety, and depression. Conversely, forgiveness can lead to improved mental health outcomes, including reduced stress and anxiety levels, improved mood, and greater overall well-being.

Better physical health: Studies have shown that forgiveness can have positive effects on physical health as well. People who practice forgiveness have lower blood pressure, reduced rates of heart disease, and improved immune function compared to those who hold onto grudges.

Improved relationships: Forgiveness can also lead to improved relationships with others. When we forgive someone who has wronged us, we can build stronger and more meaningful relationships based on trust, understanding, and mutual respect.

Increased happiness: Forgiveness can also lead to increased happiness and life satisfaction. When we let go of anger and resentment, we are free to focus on the positive aspects of our lives, leading to greater happiness and fulfilment.

Spiritual growth: Forgiveness is also an important component of many spiritual traditions and can help us to develop greater compassion, empathy, and understanding towards others. By practicing forgiveness, we can cultivate a deeper sense of spirituality and purpose in our lives, leading to greater personal growth and fulfilment.

Overall, forgiveness is good for you because it can improve your mental and physical health, lead to stronger relationships, increase happiness and life satisfaction, and promote spiritual growth and personal development.

The Transformative Power of Forgiveness:

Forgiveness is not only beneficial for our mental and emotional well-being; it also holds the potential to transform our lives. By releasing the heavy burdens of unforgiveness and bitterness, we create space for healing, personal growth, and improved relationships. It frees us from the negative cycle that perpetuates pain and allows us to move forward with clarity, compassion, and a renewed sense of purpose. Moreover, forgiveness enables us to break the cycle of hurt, fostering a ripple effect that extends beyond ourselves, positively impacting others.

Unforgiveness and bitterness are harbingers of stagnation and suffering. Their presence undermines personal growth, impedes progress, and restricts happiness. By understanding the consequences of holding onto these emotions and employing strategies to overcome them, we can break free from their grip. Cultivating empathy, practicing forgiveness, and prioritizing self-care pave the way for healing and transformation. Letting go of the twins of unforgiveness and bitterness enables individuals to embrace a life filled with joy, peace, and countless opportunities for growth.

How do you practice forgiveness?

Practicing forgiveness can be challenging, but it is an important skill that can lead to greater peace, happiness, and personal growth. Here are some steps you can take to practice forgiveness:

1. Acknowledge your feelings: Before you can forgive someone, it's important to acknowledge and process your own feelings of anger, hurt, or resentment. Take time to reflect on how the situation has affected you and allow yourself to feel your emotions without judgment.

2. Empathize with the other person: Try to see the situation from the other person's perspective. This can help you to understand their motivations and actions and may help you to feel more compassion towards them.

3. Choose to forgive: Forgiveness is a choice, and it's important to make a conscious decision to let go of your anger and resentment towards 4 the other person. This doesn't mean that you condone their actions or that you have to forget what happened, but it does mean that you are choosing to release the negative feelings and emotions that are holding you back.

4. Communicate your forgiveness: If possible, communicate your forgiveness to the other person. This can be done through a conversation, a letter, or even just a mental affirmation. Let them know that you have chosen to forgive them and that you are moving forward in a positive way.

5. Practice self-care: Forgiveness can be a difficult and emotional process, so it's important to practice self-care as you work through it. This may involve seeking support from friends or a therapist, engaging in stress-relieving activities like yoga or meditation, or simply taking time for yourself to rest and recharge.

Remember, forgiveness is a process, and it may take time and effort to fully let go of your anger and resentment. But by practicing forgiveness, you can experience greater peace, happiness, and personal growth in your life.

- Forgiveness is a crucial step in beginning again. Forgive yourself for any mistakes or missteps that led to feeling stuck or off-track. It is important to recognize that everyone makes mistakes, and accepting this will help lift your spirits and keep you motivated.

CHAPTER 3:

PART A THE CRAFT OF LIBERATION: SHEDDING NEGATIVITY AND PAIN TO EMBRACE FREEDOM

Release your pain and what did not work.

Releasing and forgiveness are important for personal growth and healing. Holding onto negative emotions and grudges can have a detrimental impact on our physical and mental health, as well as our relationships with others. Releasing and forgiveness can help us let go of negative emotions, heal from past hurts, and move forward in a positive direction.

Releasing refers to the process of letting go of negative emotions and thoughts that are holding us back. This may involve acknowledging and accepting our emotions, expressing them in a healthy way, and finding ways to move past them. Releasing can help us reduce stress and anxiety, improve our mood, and cultivate a greater sense of inner peace.

Forgiveness, on the other hand, involves letting go of resentment and anger towards others who have hurt us. Forgiveness does not mean forgetting or condoning the behaviour that caused the hurt, but rather choosing to let go of the negative emotions associated with it. Forgiveness can help us improve our relationships with others, reduce our own feelings of anger and resentment, and cultivate a greater sense of empathy and compassion.

In both cases, releasing and forgiveness require a willingness to be vulnerable and open to the healing process. It may involve seeking support from others, practicing self-care, and being patient and compassionate with us and others. Ultimately, releasing and forgiveness can help us let go of the past and move forward in a positive direction, allowing us to live more fulfilling and meaningful lives.

May's Story

May sat alone in her room, tears running down her face. She had just experienced a painful breakup with her long-term partner, and the pain felt unbearable. As the reality of what had happened sank in, May knew that she needed to find a way to cope with the situation and move forward.

Acceptance and acknowledgement were the first steps May needed to take. She repeated to herself, "It's okay, it had to happen." She understood that sometimes things don't work out, no matter how hard we try. May had to make peace with herself and the situation she found herself in. It wasn't easy, but she knew that dwelling on what could have been would only prolong her suffering.

May reminded herself that life is full of ups and downs. "Sometimes you lose, and sometimes you win some," she thought. Even if the mountain before her seemed immovable, May stayed anchored in the hope that a higher power was on her side. She knew that there was a right time, place, and position for everything, and she trusted that all would fall into place when the time was right.

Letting go and releasing the pain was the next challenge May faced. She needed to break free from the norm and embrace the newness that life had to offer. May recognized that she had to let go of who she was in the context of her past relationship and allow herself to grow and change. She had to invite God to invade her life, guiding and shaping her into the person she was meant to become. May understood the power of freeing herself from the entanglements of the past and embracing the possibilities that lay ahead. May learnt to live in the present and align her thoughts to the present activity. Contentment is a great gain.

Liberating the Mind from the Shackles of Unforgiveness and Bitterness: A Tale of Personal Growth

In the intricate tapestry of human emotions, two twins, Unforgiveness and Bitterness, often intertwine to hinder our progress and emotional well-being. These formidable companions persistently anchor us in the past, preventing personal growth and sabotaging our pursuit of happiness. It is imperative, therefore, to embark on a journey of self-discovery, confronting these toxic siblings head-on, to liberate our minds and embrace a brighter future.

Unforgiveness and Bitterness originate from the painful experiences of betrayal, hurt, disappointment, or perceived injustice. Like persistent shadows, they linger in our minds, nurturing negative thoughts and emotions. This emotional weight, if carried for too long, consumes our mental and physical energy, stunting our progress and draining our vitality.

Unforgiveness, the elder twin, binds us to the past, tainting our present reality. It festers within, growing stronger with each passing day, poisoning our relationships, and freezing our emotional growth. Unforgiveness hinders our ability to forgive ourselves and others, blocking the path to inner peace and healing. It relentlessly whispers in our ears, feeding our anger and resentment, blinding us to the possibilities of reconciliation and personal growth.

While Unforgiveness shackles us, Bitterness resides and thrives within the chambers of our hearts. It corrodes our ability to trust, to love, and to believe in the goodness of others and ourselves. Bitterness fuels a constant sense of victimhood, leading to a distorted perception of reality, where every action is viewed through a lens of negativity. It imprisons us within a self-reinforcing cycle, preventing us from truly experiencing joy and finding contentment.

The Path to Liberation: Release and Letting Go:

To conquer these formidable twins, one must embark on a transformative journey towards forgiveness and letting go. It is crucial to recognize that forgiveness does not imply condoning or forgetting the wrongdoing but instead freeing ourselves from the emotional burdens that hinder our progress. By acknowledging the pain, we validate our emotions, thus enabling us to reframe our experiences and constructively move forward.

Embracing Empathy: A Key to Healing:

To dismantle the stronghold of Unforgiveness and Bitterness, we must cultivate empathy and understanding. Often, the actions of others stem from their own insecurities, fears, and life experiences. By striving to understand the motivations and perspectives of those who have caused harm, we can shift the focus away from the pain itself. As we embrace empathy, forgiveness becomes an attainable endeavour, offering the promise of personal growth and healing.

Rebuilding Bridges: The Power of Reconciliation:

Rebuilding bridges shattered by hurt and betrayal is a testament to our strength and emotional growth. True reconciliation requires open and honest communication, vulnerability, and a willingness to seek common ground. This collaborative effort, fuelled by a sincere desire for resolution, can help mend broken relationships and, in turn, free us from the debilitating grips of unforgiveness and bitterness.

The journey to liberation from unforgiveness and bitterness is an arduous but necessary one. It demands introspection, self-reflection, and a conscious effort to replace negativity with compassion and understanding. As we embark on this path, we begin to reclaim our emotional well-being, remove the chains that held us captive, and embrace personal growth. By confronting these vindictive twins, we unlock the limitless potential within ourselves, paving the way for a fulfilling and harmonious future. Remember, it is within our power to be free, for the mind is the ultimate battlefield where we wage the war against the twins of unforgiveness and bitterness.

The challenges with unforgiveness

May who carry a heavy burden of unforgiveness in her heart had experienced deep pain and betrayal in the past, which had left scars that seemed impossible to heal. The wounds inflicted by others had festered within her, trapping her in a cycle of anger and resentment.

May's unforgiveness affected every aspect of her life. It poisoned her relationships, clouded her judgment, and weighed down her spirit. She carried the pain like a heavy backpack, unable to move forward or find peace within herself.

One day, May stumbled upon a quote that struck a chord deep within her soul: "Holding onto unforgiveness is like drinking poison and expecting the other person to die." Those words resonated with her, awakening a glimmer of hope. She realized that her refusal to forgive was not punishing the people who had hurt her; it was only poisoning her own well-being.

Determined to break free from the chains of unforgiveness, May embarked on a journey of self-discovery and healing. She sought guidance from a wise mentor who had walked a similar path of pain and forgiveness. The mentor shared stories of resilience, forgiveness, and the transformative power it held.

As May delved deeper into her journey, she confronted her past with courage and vulnerability. She acknowledged the pain, grief, and anger that had consumed her for far too long. Through introspection and self-reflection, she began to see the destructive patterns her unforgiveness had created in her life.

Slowly but steadily, May started to release the grip of unforgiveness. It was not an easy process. There were moments of doubt, moments when the pain resurfaced with a vengeance. Yet, she persisted. She began to practice forgiveness, not as an act of condoning or forgetting, but as a means of liberating herself from the burden she had carried for so long.

With forgiveness, May discovered a newfound freedom. As she let go of grudges and resentment, she made space for love, compassion, and understanding to enter her heart. She learned to empathize with the complexities of human nature and recognize that forgiveness was a gift she could offer herself.

Through forgiveness, May's relationships began to transform. She reconnected with estranged loved ones, extending the olive branch of forgiveness and reconciliation. While not all wounds could be mended completely, the act of forgiveness opened doors for healing and understanding.

May's journey with unforgiveness taught her invaluable lessons. She realized that forgiveness was not a sign of weakness but a testament to her strength and resilience. It allowed her to reclaim her power and choose love over bitterness. It paved the way for personal growth, healing, and a renewed sense of purpose.

As May moved forward on her journey, she carried the lessons of forgiveness in her heart. She understood that life would bring new challenges and hurts, but she now possessed the strength and wisdom to choose forgiveness as a path to inner peace. With a lighter step and a heart filled with compassion, May embraced the beauty of a life unburdened by unforgiveness, inspiring others to embark on their own journeys of forgiveness and healing.

May's transformation through the power of forgiveness was remarkable. The burden of unforgiveness that had once held her captive had been lifted, and she found herself embracing life with newfound joy and freedom.

The first change May noticed was within herself. The heavy weight of anger and resentment had been replaced by a sense of lightness and inner peace. She no longer felt controlled by the past but rather empowered by her ability to let go and move forward. The poison of unforgiveness had been replaced by the healing balm of forgiveness, allowing her heart to open to love and compassion once again.

In her relationships, May experienced a profound shift. She approached interactions with others from a place of understanding and empathy rather than judgment and bitterness. The walls that had been erected around her heart began to crumble, creating space for connection and reconciliation. Some relationships were fully restored, while others found a new level of understanding and acceptance.

May's newfound perspective also extended to herself. She began to forgive herself for the mistakes and shortcomings she had carried as burdens for far too long. Self-compassion replaced self-criticism, and she learned to embrace her own humanity with kindness and understanding. This inner forgiveness fuelled her personal growth and allowed her to pursue her dreams and passions without the weight of past failures holding her back.

As May shared her journey of forgiveness and healing with others, she became an inspiration to those who were also trapped in the cycle of unforgiveness. Her story served as a reminder that forgiveness is not a sign of weakness but a courageous act of self-liberation. She encouraged others to embark on their own paths of forgiveness, assuring them that healing, and transformation was possible.

Through workshops, speaking engagements, and even authoring a book about her experiences, May touched the lives of many. She offered practical tools and strategies for navigating the challenging terrain of forgiveness, providing a roadmap for those who were ready to embark on their own journeys.

May's life became a testament to the transformative power of forgiveness. She not only found peace and fulfilment within herself but also became an agent of positive change in the lives of others. Her journey taught her that forgiveness is not an easy path, but it is a path worth taking—a path that leads to a life filled with love, compassion, and limitless possibilities.

As May's journey continued, the ripple effects of her transformation became more apparent. People began to seek her guidance and advice, drawn to her warmth, wisdom, and authenticity. She created a community of individuals who had experienced the power of forgiveness firsthand and were now committed to living a life free from the shackles of unforgiveness.

May's workshops and speaking engagements became highly sought-after events, where attendees found solace, inspiration, and practical strategies to navigate their own forgiveness journeys. Through her storytelling and vulnerability, she created a safe space for others to share their own experiences and gain insights from one another.

In addition to her public work, May also established a support network for individuals who were struggling with forgiveness. She facilitated small group sessions where people could gather in a non-judgmental environment, share their stories, and receive guidance from both May and fellow participants. These intimate gatherings fostered deep connections and a sense of belonging, providing a valuable support system for those in need.

As time went on, May's impact reached far beyond her immediate community. Her book, chronicling her personal journey of forgiveness and providing practical tools for others, became a bestseller. Readers from all levels of society found solace in her words and embarked on their own paths of healing and forgiveness.

May's work also caught the attention of researchers and therapists, who recognized the significance of her insights and the transformative power of forgiveness. She collaborated with professionals in the field to develop evidence-based programs and resources, ensuring that her message of forgiveness could reach even more individuals in need of healing.

Through it all, May remained humble and grateful. She knew that her journey was not just about her personal healing but about creating a ripple effect of positive change in the world. Her experiences have taught her the profound impact that forgiveness can have on individuals, relationships, and society.

May's story became a testament to the power of forgiveness, inspiring countless people to release the burdens of the past and embrace a life of love, compassion, and growth. She had transformed her own pain into a source of light and healing, and in doing so, she had become a beacon of hope for others.

As May reflected on her journey, she marvelled at the transformative power of forgiveness and its ability to shape not only individual lives but also the world at large. She knew that her work was far from done and that there were still countless hearts waiting to be touched by the healing power of forgiveness.

With renewed determination, May continued to share her story, spread her message, and empower others to embark on their own journeys of forgiveness. She believed that through forgiveness, individuals could find liberation, connection, and a deeper sense of purpose. And with each person she touched, May knew that she was contributing to a more forgiving, compassionate, and harmonious world.

The Benefits of Repentance and Moving on In Life

Repentance and moving on in life can bring numerous benefits to an individual. Here are some of the key advantages:

Repentance allows individuals to confront their past mistakes and take responsibility for their actions. It provides an opportunity for self-reflection and acknowledging the pain or hurt caused to oneself or others. By seeking forgiveness and making amends, individuals can experience emotional healing and find closure, freeing themselves from the burden of guilt or regret.

Repentance also opens the door to personal growth and transformation. It involves recognizing areas where one needs to change and making a commitment to do better. Through repentance, individuals learn from their past mistakes, develop self-awareness, and strive to become more compassionate, empathetic, and morally upright individuals.

In addition, repentance plays a crucial role in repairing damaged relationships, providing an opportunity to apologize sincerely, and work towards rebuilding trust. By acknowledging their mistakes and demonstrating a genuine desire to change, individuals can mend broken bonds and restore meaningful connections with others. When individuals confront their past actions, seek forgiveness, and make amends, they can let go of the weight of guilt and find solace in the knowledge that they have taken steps towards reconciliation. This peace of mind allows them to focus on the present and future without being haunted by past mistakes.

Self-esteem and Self-worth is improved. By acknowledging their mistakes and taking responsibility for their actions, they demonstrate courage and integrity. As they work towards personal growth and positive change, they regain confidence in themselves and their ability to make better choices, leading to a healthier self-perception. Repentance fosters empathy and compassion towards others.

Repentance and moving on free individuals from the shackles of their past mistakes. It allows them to embrace the present and future with a renewed sense of purpose and determination. By letting go of the past and learning from their experiences, individuals can seize new opportunities, make positive changes, and pursue a more fulfilling and meaningful life.

In summary, repentance and moving on in life bring emotional healing, personal growth, restored relationships, peace of mind, improved self-esteem, enhanced empathy, and the chance for new opportunities. These benefits contribute to a more wholesome and fulfilling life, where individuals can learn from their past and embrace a brighter future.

- Perseverance: The ability to keep going despite challenges, setbacks, or failures is crucial. Perseverance enables individuals to learn from mistakes, grow, and find success.

CHAPTER 3:

PART B BREAKING LOOSE: ABANDONING OLD HABITS AND PATTERNS

The importance of renouncing old ties

Renouncing old ties is a powerful act of personal growth and self-discovery. It involves consciously letting go of relationships, habits, beliefs, or circumstances that no longer serve a positive purpose in our lives. Renouncing old ties is an essential step towards personal liberation, emotional well-being, and creating a more fulfilling and purposeful life.

One of the key reasons why renouncing old ties is important is because it allows individuals to explore and discover their authentic selves. In our journey towards self-discovery, it is crucial to shed outdated connections and create space for self-reflection and introspection. By renouncing old ties, we can redefine our identity and align our choices with our genuine selves.

It gives us the opportunity to understand our true desires, values, and aspirations. Holding onto negative or toxic relationships can be emotionally draining. Renouncing these ties frees us from the emotional baggage and unhealthy dynamics that may have been causing stress, anxiety, or unhappiness in our lives. It paves the way for emotional healing, self-care, and the cultivation of healthy relationships. Renouncing old ties is an act of prioritizing our emotional well-being and creating space for positive and nurturing connections. Renouncing old ties also creates room for personal growth and development. It allows us to break free from limiting beliefs, negative patterns, or comfort zones that hinder our progress.

By embracing new experiences and challenges, we can expand our horizons, acquire new skills, and evolve into the best version of ourselves. Renouncing old ties is an act of stepping into our true potential and creating a life that is aligned with our authentic selves. Another important reason to renounce old ties is the empowerment and autonomy it brings. By letting go of old ties, we take control of our lives and make choices based on our own values, aspirations, and well-being. It frees us from being influenced by external factors or the expectations of others. Renouncing old ties fosters a sense of autonomy and self-empowerment, allowing us to create a life that aligns with our true desires.

Renouncing old ties also creates space for positive connections to enter our lives. Letting go of old ties that no longer serve a positive purpose allows us to surround ourselves with like-minded individuals who uplift and encourage our personal growth. By cultivating a positive support system, we enhance our journey towards self-fulfilment and create a sense of belonging. Furthermore, renouncing old ties liberates us from the weight of the past. It releases us from the burden of holding onto relationships or situations that no longer contribute positively to our lives.

This freedom allows us to move forward, unencumbered by past attachments, and embrace new opportunities and possibilities. Renouncing old ties is about letting go of what no longer serves our growth, well-being, and happiness. It is a courageous step towards self-discovery, personal growth, and creating a life that aligns with our truest selves. In conclusion, renouncing old ties is a vital step towards personal growth, emotional well-being, and living a fulfilling life. It involves consciously letting go of relationships, habits, beliefs, or circumstances that no longer contribute positively to our journey. By renouncing old ties, we create room for self-discovery, emotional healing, personal growth, and positive connections. It is a courageous act that paves the way for personal transformation and a brighter future. So, take the leap, let go of what no longer serves you, and embrace the path towards a more authentic and fulfilling existence.

- Take time to reflect.

CHAPTER 4:

RESURGENCE OF A FRESH START: REDISCOVERING YOUR IDENTITY AND REGAINING CONFIDENCE

Throughout our journey, we all encounter moments that push us towards a fresh start. This chapter delves into the concept of resurgence – the act of rediscovering your identity and regaining confidence. Attention Feeling lost and doubtful can often consume our lives. Whether due to personal setbacks, professional challenges, or simply the ebb and flow of life's uncertainty, we can find ourselves questioning who we truly are and doubting our abilities.

Fortunately, the path to a resurgence lies within each one of us – a renewed chance to redefine ourselves and regain the confidence that once propelled us forward. Interest Rediscovering your identity is an introspective process that requires stepping away from external influences and embracing self-reflection. It is an opportunity to sort through the clutter and noise, reconnect with your true essence, and uncover the passions that once ignited your soul. Doing so opens the door to reignite your purpose and align your actions with your authentic self.

Rediscovering Your Identity, The journey towards rediscovering your identity starts with introspection. Take the time to reflect on your values, 1 belief, and aspirations. Ask yourself: Who am I? For what do I stand? What brings me joy? Dive deep into your past experiences and memories, analysing the moments that shaped you and the lessons you have learned along the way. Another powerful tool is self-expression. Engaging in creative outlets such as writing, painting, or dancing can help you tap into the subconscious and unlock hidden aspects of your identity. Allow yourself to explore without judgment and let your authentic self-emerge.

Regaining Confidence As you embark on the journey of rediscovering your identity, regaining confidence becomes a natural byproduct. Remember, confidence is not merely about having an inflated ego; it is about acknowledging your worth and embracing the challenges that 2 lie ahead. One way to boost confidence is through self-care. Taking care of your physical, mental, and emotional well-being reinforces a positive self-image.

Engaging in activities that make you feel good, such as exercise, meditation, or spending time in nature, can help you reconnect with your inner strength and enhance overall confidence. Surrounding yourself with positivity is crucial. In times of self-doubt, seek support from friends, family, or even professional mentors who can provide guidance and encouragement.

By surrounding yourself with individuals who uplift and inspire you, you create a safe space to rebuild your confidence and regain a sense of purpose. Action To foster resurgence and maintain your fresh start, it is essential to act. Create a plan and set achievable goals aligned with your newfound identity. Break them down into smaller milestones, allowing yourself to build confidence with each step forward.

Celebrate your successes along the way, no matter how small. Additionally, embrace the power of gratitude. Taking time daily to acknowledge and appreciate the good in your life can shift your mindset, promote positivity, and fuel your confidence.

Gratitude helps you stay in touch with your new identity, reminding you of the progress you have made and the hurdles you have overcome. Conclusion The path to resurgence is a personal journey filled with moments of self-discovery, reflection, and growth.

By rediscovering your identity and regaining confidence, you can break free from self-doubt and transcend the limitations that hold you back. Embrace this opportunity for change and unleash your full potential. Remember, a fresh start is not just a chance to rewrite your story; it is an invitation to reclaim your true self and live a fulfilling life. Embrace the resurgence, embark on the journey towards your restored identity, and regain confidence.

BEGIN AGAIN – "Change is the only constant."

If you are not attracting success, wealth, good relationships, a lengthy career, or any desired outcomes - change your philosophy. Jim Rohn

In the journey of beginning again, there is always a storm that precedes it. It starts with a faint rumble in the distance, like a whisper in the wind, gradually growing louder until it becomes an undeniable force that shakes the very foundation of your existence. This storm serves as the announcement, the wake-up call that tells you it is time to start afresh.

As you stand at the verge of this new chapter, you realize that protecting your peace becomes crucial. The storm demands your full attention and commitment to change. You must be willing to walk away from anything in your life that no longer serves a purpose, even if it means making difficult and heart-wrenching choices along the way. Being decisive, focused, and setting boundaries are all essential in this process of shedding the old and embracing the new.

But it is not just about letting go and walking away; it also requires you to forgive and love unconditionally. You must be intentional and resilient in your pursuit of a fresh start. Kindness and sensitivity become virtues you must possess, along with wisdom and discernment. Honouring yourself in every way and knowing who you truly are becomes paramount.

Understanding your purpose and fully embracing it becomes vital in this new beginning. You must be determined to create the life you envision, cultivating traits such as discipline, perseverance, and the refusal to give up. Moments of doubt and challenges will undoubtedly arise, but it is your faith that becomes your guiding force. It enables you to dance and sing through the storm, celebrating the victory that lies beyond.

Connecting with your source daily and taking time to care for yourself become activities that bring balance and strength. Amidst the chaos, you find solace and clarity. You realize that you are not just beginning again for yourself; you are doing it for those around you. You must let your inner light shine, uplifting those who have been affected by the storm. Your beginning again is not just about personal growth; it encompasses advocating for the less fortunate and giving voice to the voiceless.

Being resilient, creative, and sensitive are qualities that will enable you to make a real impact and bring about positive change. You become an agent of transformation, a beacon of hope amidst the darkness. And finally, to truly be the change, you must become the storm itself, the force that brings about the necessary upheaval for a new beginning. A force of change, altering the very fabric of the world around us.

In the end, beginning again is a journey of transformation - a testament to the possibilities that lie within each of us. It calls upon our faith, resilience, and determination to overcome the storms of life. It is through this journey that we learn to protect our peace, embrace our true selves, and fulfil our purpose. So, let us embark on this captivating journey, knowing that beyond the storm lies a new dawn, where victory, self-discovery, and the power to make a difference await us.

It is not to be taken lightly, for it demands your unwavering commitment and dedication. The length of this narration allows for a deep exploration of the themes and concepts surrounding embarking on a fresh start. Each word carries significance and weight, urging you to embrace the storm and emerge stronger on the other side.

May's Path

May had been struggling for the past few months. She had been trying her hardest to stay optimistic and keep her life going, but the reality of her current situation was slowly wearing her down. On the outside, she was still doing her usual activities: going to work, seeing her friends, and taking care of her family. On the inside, though, she felt exhausted and confused, her motivation slipping away.

Since she was a child, May had been a dreamer. She could get lost in her own visions and thoughts, but now those dreams felt like a distant memory, forgotten in the darkness of her mind. She felt as if she was stuck in an endless cycle, taking one step forward and two steps back. Every day was increasingly more difficult. She was frustrated and scared, unsure of what to do next.

May looked out her window at the grey sky and the rain that had been falling for days now. All she wanted was a sign, something to break the monotony and give her a hint of the future. But nothing came. The only thing that seemed certain was her growing doubt and insecurity. She felt completely lost.

Finally, after hours of deep thinking, something shifted in May's mind. She realized that no matter how hard it seemed, she still had the power to take the first step towards a brighter future. She had to start by taking care of herself. It would be slow and inconvenient, but it was the only way. May took a deep breath and started to make her plans. She wrote them down and shared them with her trusted friends and family. Little by little, she started.

May had been struggling for the past few months, her mental well-being feeling increasingly fragile. It was as if, without her realising, she had stopped believing in her own purpose, in what she was doing with her life. She hadn't the courage to take the risk and make a change, so instead she was stuck in a downward spiral of doubt and insecurity.

May had been chatting with Chris, one of her coworkers, and realized that Chris was feeling similarly stuck. Despite having worked hard to get her dream job, she felt completely unfulfilled. Her work felt meaningless, and she had a nagging feeling that there must be something else out there, something more rewarding.

May sympathized deeply with Chris and could relate to her feelings of stagnation and aimlessness. She knew how it felt to be at a crossroads, not knowing which path to take or what the future would bring. She wanted to help Chris see what she already saw in herself - that if she took the first step towards something new, it could lead to amazing things. So, May, decided to encourage Chris by sharing her own story of doubt and insecurity and by pointing her towards resources like books, podcasts and articles on topics related to personal development. May suggested that Chris read "The Power of Now" by Eckhart Tolle as a way of helping her come back into the present moment and start making positive changes in her life from there.

At first, Chris was unsure about taking such big steps all at once, but as May continued talking about the potential rewards that come from being brave enough to face our fears, something changed inside of her.

Chris finally saw how far she had come already despite all the doubts she was facing; giving up wasn't an option anymore; instead, now was the time for action! She thanked May for being so honest and inspiring in their conversation and said goodbye, eager to start planning right away!

As time passed, May and Chris were approached by Tendo, a young man who had been feeling left out and isolated. He told them that he didn't know what his purpose in life was, and he felt like no one understood him. May and Chris were taken aback by how similar his struggle was to their own. They could feel the desperation radiating from him and couldn't help but feel empathy for him.

May invited Tendo to join their conversation about personal growth and development, hoping it would help him see that he wasn't alone in his struggles. As they talked, May, recognised within herself the same doubts and fears that she had seen in Chris - of not knowing where your life is going or what you genuinely want. And yet, despite that uncertainty, being brave enough to take a risk can bring rewards beyond imagination. Tendo was so inspired by the stories of bravery that both Chris and May shared with him, so much so that before saying goodbye, he asked if there was any way they could stay in touch because he wanted to keep up with their journey and hopefully learn from it himself.

The three of them exchanged numbers before leaving, making plans to meet up again soon for another inspiring chat on personal growth and development. The energy around them as they parted ways was tangible - everyone shared an unspoken understanding that each of their struggles had been given new meaning through their shared experience.

May and Chris began to open to each other and to Tendo. The three of them would spend hours talking and laughing, sharing their stories, and offering each other much needed support and understanding. As May and Chris began to open their hearts to each other, they finally started to feel the relief they had been seeking for so long.

Thanks to Tendo, May and Chris finally felt like they weren't alone in life. They had found their own purpose, not just in work but in the joy of loving one another. May and Chris started reflecting on their journey and realised how far they had come since that fateful encounter with Tendo. They both appreciated the courage it took for him to approach them, sparking a newfound appreciation for each other. Through his example, they both found new strength and hope, even in the face of uncertainty.

As they continued to meet up and share stories with Tendo, May and Chris began to feel more connected than ever before. They began to understand the importance of being vulnerable with one another and were able to start finding ways to truly support each other on their paths towards personal growth and development.

Their meetings went from a once-a-week thing to an almost daily occurrence as Tendo became a part of their lives, helping them appreciate the insignificant things, such as going out for dinner or taking a walk together. He was no longer just a chance acquaintance or passing figure; he had become someone who was deeply important to them both.

Tendo had brought so much positivity into their lives, and it seemed like fate when he eventually found his own purpose - running his own business in the field of marketing. May and Chris couldn't have been happier for him; seeing him find his callings made them realise that anything is possible if you keep pushing yourself forward, no matter what the obstacles are.

May and Chris's friendship continued growing stronger day by day until, eventually, they decided that no matter what life threw at them, they would always be there for each other - like two rocks standing firm against any storm that might come crashing down upon them. And though Tendo would soon have other commitments due to his work, May, knew deep down he would always be there when she needed him most.

Rediscovering one's identity is a crucial step in making a fresh start and regaining confidence because it allows individuals to:

Identity: Rediscovering one's identity involves deep introspection and self-reflection. It prompts individuals to reevaluate their values, beliefs, passions, talents, and aspirations. This process helps them better understand themselves, their priorities, and what truly makes them happy. By knowing who they are, individuals can align their lives with their authentic selves, which boosts their self-confidence and provides a solid foundation for a fresh start.

Some researchers state that reconnecting with one's cultural heritage impact the process of rediscovering one's identity. Reconnecting with one's cultural heritage often involves learning about the traditions, values, customs, and history of a particular group. By understanding and appreciating these aspects, individuals can develop a sense of pride in their own cultural identity. This pride acts as a building block for confidence, as it reinforces feelings of self-worth and promotes a positive self-image. Sense of belonging, self-discovery, validation and acceptance, cultural wisdom and resilience contributes to a stronger self-identity and confidence.

Letting go of the past: Sometimes, people lose their sense of identity due to past trauma, negative experiences, or societal expectations. Rediscovering one's identity provides an opportunity to let go of those past influences and break free from their limitations. It allows individuals to redefine themselves based on their own terms rather than being defined by external factors. This process enables them to leave the baggage of the past behind and approach new beginnings with a fresh perspective.

Setting new goals and direction: Rediscovering one's identity often leads to a revaluation of personal goals, aspirations, and dreams. It helps individuals align their life choices and actions with their true desires. By establishing new goals and charting a new direction, individuals regain a sense of purpose and motivation. This renewed focus provides a clear path forward, contributing to their confidence in their abilities to achieve their aspirations.

Embracing authenticity: When individuals rediscover their authentic self, it empowers them to embrace who they truly are. They no longer feel the need to conform to societal norms or make choices solely to please others. Embracing authenticity allows individuals to express their true thoughts, feelings, and perspectives. This genuine self-expression not only contributes to their self-confidence but also attracts people and opportunities that align with their true selves, leading to a more fulfilling and successful fresh start.

Building resilience: The process of rediscovering one's identity requires self-compassion, courage, and resilience. It involves facing fears, embracing vulnerabilities, and overcoming obstacles. By going through this process, individuals develop resilience and inner strength. This newfound resilience allows them to navigate challenges and setbacks more effectively, which in turn boosts their confidence in their ability to handle any obstacles that may arise in their fresh start journey. In summary, rediscovering one's identity plays a vital role in making a fresh start and regaining confidence by enabling self-reflection, letting go of the past, setting new goals, embracing authenticity, and building resilience. It empowers individuals to live authentically and align their actions with their true selves, leading to a more confident and fulfilling life.

Why is it necessary to begin again in life?

There are countless moments where the need to rephrase our journey becomes not just beneficial but imperative. Why, you ask? Because starting anew opens doors to personal growth, learning from past missteps, and carving a path that leads to a brighter destination. Let us explore the reasons why beginning again is truly a life-altering endeavour.

Firstly, change is an ever-present facet of life. It swoops upon us in unexpected ways, leaving us no choice but to reset our course. Whether it be the loss of a job, venturing into unfamiliar territory, or the end of a cherished relationship, change can be gruelling. However, there are strategies to navigate this tumultuous sea. Focus on what you can control, for it is through these actions that a semblance of power is regained. Adaptability, is the ability to embrace fresh ideas and malleable approaches, is crucial. Stay positive and let your optimism anchor you through the storm. Transparent communication serves as a beacon to guide you and those around you through times of change. And tend to yourself. Protect your mind and body, providing the necessary sustenance to weather the storm. Seek support from loved ones or professionals if the grasp of overwhelming emotions becomes too tight.

Secondly, beginning again presents an opportunity for growth, both personally and professionally. Reflect upon past missteps with unyielding honesty. Cultivating self-awareness is the key to unlocking the gates of profound personal discovery. Identify your strengths, weaknesses, values, and areas in need of improvement. Learn from failures, for they are stepping stones towards growth. Embrace continuous learning and development, for our minds, are sponges yearning for knowledge. Surround yourself with individuals who wholeheartedly support and encourage your journey towards growth. Seek mentors, coaches, and friends who will shine a light on your path and offer guidance when needed.

In conclusion, embarking on a journey to rephrase one's narrative embodies resilience, determination, and the unwavering belief in the potential for a better future. Remember that falling seven times only strengthens the resolve to rise an eighth. Failure is merely a detour on the road to success, a lesson rather than a permanent state. Normalize the concept of beginning again and allow it to permeate society's fabric. Redefine your journey, leaving behind whatever hinders your progress. The power to change your life is within your grasp. Identify who you are, your purpose, your destination, and the steps required to reach it. As formal as these words may be, they carry a profound message of hope and renewal. Embrace the concept of beginning again and set forth on a path of transformation.

Steps to Beginning Again.

Beginning again can be a challenging process, but there are steps you can take to help make it a smoother and more successful transition.

Tendo had to follow some steps, and you can follow them too.

The sun peeked through the clouds, its rays giving a much-needed warmth to the day. Standing on the wide street, surrounded by unfamiliar faces, Tendo felt a twinge of anxiety. He had been in this exact spot before, but it felt different now. It was as if he was a different person, a recent version of himself. This feeling of starting over was both daunting and exciting.

Tendo took a deep breath and reminded himself that he was ready for this. He had taken the necessary steps to get himself back on track, and he was determined to make it work. As he began to stride forward, he recalled all the advice he had received from his friends and family. He was ready to accept the challenge and embark on this new journey.

The first step was to recognize the things he had to let go of to move forward. Tendo was determined to leave his old life behind and start fresh. He knew that to do this, he would have to make some tough decisions and take some hard steps. He was ready to make the necessary changes and become a better version of himself.

He was ready for the challenge, and with a newfound determination, he continued walking down the street, a new beginning awaiting him. To get back on track, you must first take a step back and assess your current situation. What challenges are you currently facing? What has brought you to this place in life? By identifying the obstacles that may have led to your current state, you can then strategize ways to overcome them. Once these solutions are identified, it is important to create achievable goals that work toward these solutions and provide motivation for achieving them. Additionally, it is important to enlist the help of family and friends or seek advice from professionals when necessary. Lastly, utilize resources available such as support groups or online courses/ programs to further yourself on your journey. The combination of these steps will help create a solid foundation for success going forward.

Resilience: The ability to bounce back from setbacks and adapt to change is crucial. Resilient individuals are better equipped to navigate challenges and maintain a positive outlook.

CHAPTER 5:

RESURGENCE OF A FRESH START: RESOLVING TO BEGIN AGAIN, RETREAT

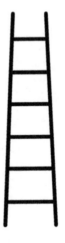

You have come to a place leaving some things, Resolve, BEGIN AGAIN

Resolve, or determination, is important when starting over because it helps you stay focused and motivated towards your goals. When beginning again, you may face challenges or setbacks that can make it easy to become discouraged or give up. However, having a strong resolve can help you persevere through these difficulties and stay committed to achieving your objectives.

Resolve refers to the determination, firmness, and commitment to achieving a particular goal or making a positive change in one's life. It involves an intense sense of purpose and the willingness to take action and persevere despite obstacles or setbacks. When we talk about resolving to make a change, it means making a firm decision to address certain aspects of our lives that may no longer align with our values, desires, or well-being.

Retreating from the norm, in this context, means intentionally stepping away from the familiar or routine aspects of our lives. It involves creating a space, whether physically or mentally, where we can detach ourselves from the daily distractions, pressures, and expectations of society or our usual environments. By retreating, we create an opportunity for self-reflection, introspection, and a break from the habits and patterns that may have held us back or contributed to a sense of stagnation.

When we come to a place and leave some things behind, it signifies a conscious decision to let go of certain aspects of our lives that no longer serve us positively. It could involve leaving behind limiting beliefs, toxic relationships, unfulfilling jobs, or any other circumstances that hinder our growth, well-being, or confidence.

By releasing these burdens, we create space for new opportunities, personal growth, and a fresh start.

Begin again with resolve represents the start of a new chapter in our lives. It is a commitment to approach our journey with determination, courage, and self-belief. It is about regaining our confidence, rediscovering our strengths, and redefining our priorities and goals. Beginning again with resolve allows us to tap into our inner power, set new intentions, and take inspired actions towards creating the life we desire.

In summary, the concept of Resolve and Retreating from the norm involves making a firm decision to address certain aspects of our lives, intentionally stepping away from our usual environments, leaving behind what no longer serves us, and starting anew with confidence and determination. It is a transformative process that empowers us to reclaim our lives, embrace change, and create a future that aligns with our true selves.

Evelyn's journey to Resolve, taking a step back to come to a place of leaving some things and BEGIN AGAIN and Regaining her confidence.

Evelyn found herself feeling stuck and dissatisfied with her life. She had been following a routine that no longer brought her joy or fulfilment. She yearned for something more, but she wasn't sure how to make a change. One day, Evelyn came across a book that spoke to her soul. It was about the power of resolve and retreating from the norm. Intrigued by the idea of reclaiming her life and regaining her confidence, she decided to embark on a journey of self-discovery.

Evelyn took a step back from her daily routine and found a quiet retreat nestled in the serene countryside. Surrounded by nature's beauty, she created a space for introspection and reflection. In this peaceful environment, Evelyn began to let go of the things that were holding her back. She realized that she had been carrying the weight of self-doubt and fear for far too long. Evelyn resolved to release these burdens, acknowledging that they no longer served her journey. With each passing day, she shed limiting beliefs and negative self-talk, making room for self-acceptance and self-love to blossom.

During her retreat, Evelyn immersed herself in activities that sparked her joy and passion. She painted, wrote, and explored new hobbies. Through these creative endeavours, she discovered her inner strength and rekindled her lost confidence. Evelyn realized that she had talents and dreams that were waiting to be nurtured and pursued.

As Evelyn began to feel a renewed sense of purpose and clarity, she made a commitment to herself to embrace change and create a life aligned with her authentic desires. She set new goals and crafted a vision for her future—one that encompassed her passions, values, and personal growth. With her resolve guiding her, Evelyn returned from her retreat with a newfound confidence and a determination to make positive changes in her life. She surrounded herself with supportive and like-minded individuals who uplifted and encouraged her along the way.

Evelyn took practical steps towards her goals, breaking free from the limitations that had held her back in the past. She pursued further education, started a creative business, and nurtured meaningful relationships. Through the ups and downs, Evelyn remained steadfast in her resolve, knowing that setbacks were merely opportunities for growth and learning.

Over time, Evelyn's journey of resolve and regaining her confidence bore fruit. She blossomed into a confident, empowered woman who lived authentically and pursued her passions. Her journey inspired others to embark on their own paths of self-discovery and transformation.

And so, Evelyn's story serves as a reminder that by retreating from the norm, leaving behind what no longer serves us, and beginning again with resolve, we can regain our confidence, embrace change, and create a life filled with purpose, fulfilment, and joy.

Evelyn found herself feeling stuck and dissatisfied with her life. She had been following a routine that no longer brought her joy or fulfilment. She yearned for something more, but she wasn't sure how to make a change.

One day, Evelyn stumbled upon an old journal from her teenage years. As she flipped through the pages filled with her dreams and aspirations, she realized how much she had lost sight of herself over the years. Inspired by her younger self's passion and determination, Evelyn decided to embark on a journey of self-discovery and renewal.

Evelyn knew that to rediscover herself and regain her confidence, she needed to retreat from the familiar and create space for introspection. She booked a week-long stay at a serene mountain retreat, surrounded by towering trees and peaceful solitude. It was a place where she could disconnect from the outside world and reconnect with her innermost desires.

During her retreat, Evelyn spent her days immersed in nature, taking long walks through the forest, and sitting by the tranquil lake. She let her mind wander, reflecting on her past, her present, and the future she wanted to create. She delved into her passions, indulging in painting, writing, and playing the piano activities she had neglected for far too long.

As Evelyn spent time alone, she confronted her fears and insecurities. She recognized the negative thought patterns and self-doubt that had held her back for years. With a newfound determination, she resolved to let go of these self-imposed limitations and replace them with empowering beliefs and self-acceptance.

The retreat became a turning point for Evelyn. She realized that she had been living her life for others, conforming to societal expectations, and suppressing her true desires. It was time to break free from those chains and begin again on her own terms.

Armed with a renewed sense of purpose, Evelyn returned from her retreat and started making changes in her life. She enrolled in a photography course, reigniting her love for capturing moments of beauty. She also sought out a supportive community of like-minded individuals who shared her passions and aspirations.

With each small step, Evelyn regained her confidence and felt a renewed sense of purpose. She started a blog where she shared her artistic creations and personal journey, inspiring others to embrace their own paths of self-discovery. She began to attract opportunities that aligned with her newfound authenticity and passion.

As time went on, Evelyn's life transformed in ways she had never imagined. She launched her own photography business, capturing the beauty of nature and of people's lives and helping them see their own worth through her lens. She surrounded herself with a supportive network of friends and loved ones who celebrated her growth and encouraged her every step of the way.

Evelyn's journey to resolve, retreat, and regain her confidence was not without its challenges. She faced moments of doubt and setbacks, but she embraced them as opportunities for growth and learning. Through it all, she remained committed to her authentic self and never lost sight of the courage and determination that had brought her to this point.

In the end, Evelyn's story serves as a reminder that it is never too late to embark on a journey of self-discovery and regain one's confidence. By retreating from the norm, leaving behind what no longer serves us, and beginning again with resolve, we can create a life that is true to our passions, values, and aspirations. And in doing so, we can inspire others to do the same.

Resolve is also important because it helps you maintain a positive attitude and a growth mindset. Instead of giving up when faced with obstacles, a strong resolve allows you to view them as opportunities to learn and grow and to find creative solutions to overcome them. This can be especially important when starting over in a new direction or pursuing a new goal, as it may require you to step outside of your comfort zone and face new challenges.

Finally, having a strong resolve can be empowering and can help you build confidence in yourself and your abilities. By setting goals and working towards them with determination, you can develop a sense of accomplishment and self-worth, which can be incredibly valuable when starting over.

In short, resolve is important when starting over because it helps you stay focused, motivated, and positive and can ultimately lead to greater success and personal growth.

In summary, Resolve and retreating from the norm are interconnected concepts that encompass making a firm decision to address aspects of our lives that no longer align with our well-being, detaching ourselves from familiar routines and expectations, and leaving behind what no longer serves us positively. By doing so, we create space for personal growth, self-reflection, and the opportunity to begin again with determination and confidence. It is a transformative process that allows us to redefine our goals, rediscover our strengths, and create a life that aligns with our true selves.

CHAPTER 6:

REKINDLING AND RECONNECTING: EMBRACING FLAWS, RECLAIMING AUTHENTICITY

Revival and Reconnection

Revival and Reconnection - two powerful concepts that hold the key to a fulfilling and authentic life. In a world that often demands perfection and conformity, it is crucial to acknowledge our flaws and embrace our imperfections. It is through this process that we can truly reconnect with ourselves, reset our timelines, and restore what has been lost.

To begin this journey of revival, we must first pick ourselves up from the lows and setbacks that life has thrown our way. It is in these moments of despair that we have the opportunity to rebuild and reenergize ourselves. By filling the gap with new energy and positive affirmations, we can empower ourselves to overcome any obstacle and face the future with confidence. However, this process of revitalization goes beyond just picking ourselves up. It requires us to embrace and acknowledge the imperfect side of who we are. Often, society tells us that flaws are something to be ashamed of, but it is in accepting and embracing these imperfections that we can truly reclaim our authenticity.

By doing so, we can inspire others to do the same, creating a ripple effect of self-acceptance and authenticity. Furthermore, rekindling and reconnecting with our authentic selves requires us to get in touch with our inner beings. In a world that is constantly bombarding us with external stimuli, it becomes easy to lose sight of who we truly are. Taking time for introspection and self-reflection allows us to tune out the noise and connect with our core values and desires. By doing so, we can align our actions with our authentic selves and experience a greater sense of fulfilment.

Additionally, the process of revival and reconnection calls for the exchange of emotions. Often, we bury our true feelings, putting on a facade to fit societal norms or to please others. However, this only leads to a disconnect between our inner selves and the external world. To truly rekindle and reconnect, we must allow ourselves to be vulnerable and express our true emotions. Only then can we build genuine connections and foster relationships that are rooted in authenticity. Moreover, as we embark on this journey of revival and reconnection, it is crucial to discern between the good and the bad.

We must keep the lessons learned from our past experiences, cherishing the wisdom gained along the way. At the same time, we must learn to let go of negative patterns and behaviours that no longer serve us. By keeping the good and shedding the bad, we are able to create space for personal growth and transformation. In the process of reviving our spirits, we must not neglect the needs of our physical bodies.

True revival comes when we prioritize our well-being and make choices that nourish both our mind and body. By engaging in activities that bring us joy and practicing self-care, we can revive our bodies and allow our spirits to soar. Finally, rekindling and reconnecting is not just about the relationship we have with ourselves. It is also about the connections we form with others.

As humans, we are social beings who thrive on genuine connections. By embracing our flaws and reclaiming our authenticity, we allow others to do the same. Through empathy and understanding, we build deeper connections that foster growth, support, and a sense of belonging. The journey of revival and reconnection is a lifelong process that requires us to embrace our flaws and reclaim our authenticity. By picking ourselves up, embracing our imperfections, getting in touch with our inner beings, expressing our true emotions, discerning between the good and the bad, reviving our bodies and spirits, and building genuine connections, we can experience a more fulfilled and meaningful life. So, let us embark on this journey together, embracing our flaws and reclaiming our authenticity.

Embracing flaws and reclaiming authenticity is a personal journey.

Recognizing that everyone has flaws and imperfections is one of the steps in reclaiming your authenticity. Embrace the flaws and remind yourself that they do not define your worth or authenticity. We live in a society that has unrealistic standards and expectations on individuals, therefor, one must focus on what truly matters and let go of the pressure to fulfil societal norms.

It is essential to treat yourself with kindness, understanding, and forgiveness when you make mistakes or fall short of expectations. Authenticity requires vulnerability and the willingness to show yourself as you truly are, including your flaws. Be open about your imperfections and embrace the courage to be vulnerable, as it can lead to genuine connections with others.

Surround yourself with individuals who nurture and value your true self. Seek out relationships with friends and loved ones who accept your flaws and celebrate your authenticity. Instead of striving for perfection, prioritize personal growth and self-improvement. Embrace your flaws as opportunities to learn, develop, and become a better version of yourself. This mindset shift can help you embrace authenticity and continue evolving.

Engage in self-reflection to understand your values, passions, and desires. Allow yourself the freedom to express who you truly are without fear of judgment. This could involve engaging in creative outlets, sharing your thoughts and feelings with trusted individuals, or exploring new activities that align with your authentic self.

Remember, embracing flaws and reclaiming authenticity is a continuous journey. Be patient with yourself, celebrate small victories, and have faith that the pursuit of authenticity brings greater happiness and fulfilment in life.

However, pressures for perfection, coming from society has the potential to hinder individuals from embracing their flaws. It creates unrealistic expectations for individuals, making them believe that flaws are unacceptable and should be hidden or corrected. This leads to some individuals becoming overly critical of themselves. To some it is fear of judgment preventing them from embracing their flaws openly, they worry about being seen as inadequate. Social media edited images of others, can lead some people to self-comparison, and these individuals feel even more insecure about their flaws and less likely to embrace them. In some circumstances, low self-esteem and having unrealistic expectations of oneself are a result of society pressure.

An Honest Conversation with Yourself

As the sun set over the horizon, casting a warm glow, Sarah found herself sitting in her favourite bench in the park. It had been a long and challenging day, but she needed this time alone to reflect on her journey so far. With a deep breath, she opened her journal and began to write.

Reflecting on her past experiences was like peering into a mirror of her soul. It was a way for Sarah to understand where she had been and how far she had come. She started by revisiting her previous attempts at moving forward in life, reliving the moments that both filled her with joy and brought her to her knees.

In her reflection, Sarah acknowledged the mistakes she had made. She realized that these mistakes were not failures but rather steppingstones on the path to success. Each misstep had taught her invaluable lessons and allowed her to grow both personally and professionally. It was through these experiences that she discovered her true passions and purpose.

As Sarah delved deeper into her reflection, she began to realize the importance of accountability. She took ownership of her actions, acknowledging that she was responsible for her own happiness and success. No longer could she blame external circumstances or rely solely on others for her fulfilment. It was time for her to be accountable to herself.

Sarah's reflection extended to the skills she had acquired along the way. She marvelled at her newfound resilience, courage, and determination. These qualities had been forged in the fires of adversity, and they had given her the strength to face any challenge that came her way. With each passing day, she had become a woman who could conquer the world.

But reflection was not just about the past. Sarah turned her thoughts to the present, recognizing that she was currently stuck in a rut. It was an unsettling feeling, like being trapped in quicksand, unable to move forward. She knew that her reflection would be futile if she did not take action in the present moment.

Why was she stuck? Sarah pondered this question, her pen poised over the paper. Was it fear? Lack of clarity? Or perhaps a deep-rooted belief that she was not worthy of success? It was time for an honest conversation with herself to uncover the barriers that were holding her back.

With a newfound sense of determination, Sarah made a promise to herself. She would no longer allow her past mistakes, fears, or doubts to dictate her future. She would embrace the challenges that lay ahead, knowing that with each step, she was inching closer to her dreams.

Reflecting on where she was, Sarah acknowledged that she had come a long way. She celebrated her achievements, no matter how small they seemed. She realized that progress was not always linear and that setbacks were just detours on the road to success.

As the moon rose in the night sky, Sarah closed her journal and stood up, ready to face the world once more. The honest conversation she had with herself had ignited a fire within her soul. No longer would she be a victim of her circumstances. Instead, she would be the hero of her own story, accountable to herself.

With a renewed sense of purpose and determination, Sarah took a deep breath and took her first step forward. The path ahead was uncertain, but she knew that as long as she continued to reflect and hold herself accountable, she would unlock the doors to an extraordinary future.

And so, with the moon as her witness, Sarah embarked on a new chapter of her life. A chapter filled with hope, optimism, and the unwavering belief that she had the power to create the life she truly desired.

Relating with You: Finding Beauty from Within

In the realm of relationships, it is often said that "What you do, the way you think, makes you beautiful." While I do not claim to be a relationship guru, I have gained valuable insights over time and life experiences. One such insight is the profound impact that our closest relationships have on our lives. They can either lift us up or bring us down.

Take a moment to reflect on the past five or ten years of your life. Grab a pen and a piece of paper and jot down the traits and qualities you see. Are you pleased with what you find? The people we surround ourselves with shape our character and influence our actions. As the saying goes, we are the average of the five people we spend the most time with. So, it is crucial to evaluate the impact these individuals have had on us. Now, consider the present moment.

Who is presently in your life, and where are you on your personal journey? Do you still have the same people around you? More importantly, are you content with your current state? This self-reflection is essential in understanding the dynamics of your relationships and the effect they have on your growth. Regardless of the outcome, it is crucial to recognize our own role in our successes or shortcomings. Take some time to reflect on the time you have spent with these individuals and the conversations you have had together. This introspection will reveal the reasons for your current situation. Perhaps you have allowed negative influences to hold you back, or maybe you have surrounded yourself with positivity and have achieved great things as a result.

Acknowledging your own part in this equation is the first step towards building healthier and more fulfilling relationships. Now, let's turn our attention to your new beginning. Who are you starting over with, and why? It is essential to understand that relationships, like seasons, have their own natural ebb and flow. Sometimes, letting go of what no longer serves us is the key to embracing new opportunities and embarking on a fresh journey. It may be difficult and painful to let go, but trusting the process is imperative.

Holding on to what has already served its purpose will only prevent you from embracing what truly belongs to you. It is important to note that new beginnings may not always appear glamorous from the outset. Just like a butterfly emerges from a humble cocoon, beautiful transformations often arise from unassuming beginnings.

Embrace the process of growth, even if it initially seems uncertain or challenging. The caterpillar's journey to becoming a butterfly may not be easy, but the end result is undeniably breathtaking. In conclusion, our relationships play a fundamental role in shaping our lives. They can either elevate us or hold us back. Taking the time to evaluate the people who surround us and their impact on our well-being is essential for personal growth. Likewise, recognizing our own contribution to the state of our relationships allows us to take responsibility for our actions and pave the way for healthier connections.

Embracing new beginnings, even in their early stages, opens the door to transformative possibilities. So go forth and cultivate relationships that bring out the beauty within you.

Relating with Others

Relationships are a fundamental aspect of our lives. Whether they are with family, friends, or romantic partners, relationships shape who we are and how we experience the world. Balancing personal growth with family growth is a challenge that many individuals face. On one hand, we have our own goals, dreams, and desires that we want to pursue. However, we also have responsibilities and commitments to our loved ones. Finding a harmonious balance between our personal aspirations and the needs of our family can often be daunting.

However, it is not impossible. Managing expectations is another crucial aspect of maintaining healthy relationships. Often, we enter into relationships with certain expectations of how the other person should behave, what they should provide, and how they should make us feel. However, these expectations can lead to disappointment and resentment if they are not communicated and managed effectively. It is important to have open and honest conversations with our loved ones about our expectations, as well as being willing to compromise and adjust them as needed. Remember, relationships are a two-way street, and it is essential to give as much as we receive.

People in our world come from diverse backgrounds, cultures, and experiences, which can make relationships both challenging and enriching. It is important to approach people with empathy, understanding, and respect. Instead of judging others based on our own biases or preconceived notions, we should strive to see them as individuals with unique perspectives and stories. By embracing diversity and embracing the differences that exist between us, we can build stronger and more meaningful connections with those around us.

Vulnerability is a key ingredient in establishing deep and meaningful relationships.

It involves opening up and sharing our true selves, including our fears, insecurities, and past experiences. It can be scary to let our guard down and allow others to see our vulnerabilities, but it is often in those moments of vulnerability that the strongest bonds are formed. By embracing vulnerability, we create a safe space for others to do the same, fostering trust and authenticity in our relationships. Another vital aspect of healthy relationships is refusing to seek revenge.

Conflict is inevitable in any relationship, and it is natural to feel hurt or wronged when disagreements arise. However, seeking revenge and trying to hurt the other person in return only perpetuates a vicious cycle of pain and resentment. Instead, it is essential to approach conflicts with a mindset of understanding, empathy, and forgiveness. By choosing to address issues in a constructive and respectful manner, we can work towards resolution and growth rather than perpetuating negativity.

Lastly, it is important to choose to see people beyond the mask that they present to the world. People often wear masks to protect themselves or to fit societal expectations. However, these masks can prevent us from truly knowing and connecting with each other on a deeper level. By taking the time to look beyond the surface and understand the complexities of individuals, we can create more genuine and fulfilling relationships. This involves showing curiosity, actively listening, and being non-judgmental. When we see others for who they truly are, we can appreciate their uniqueness and foster stronger connections.

In conclusion, relationships are complex and multifaceted. Balancing personal growth with family growth, managing expectations, embracing diversity, vulnerability, refusing to seek revenge, and seeing people beyond their masks are all essential ingredients for cultivating healthy and fulfilling relationships. Remember, relationships require effort, understanding, and communication. By investing in our relationships, we can create a support system that enriches our lives and helps us become the best versions of ourselves. So, let us celebrate and value the relationships that we have, and strive to build deeper connections with others.

CHAPTER 7:

REINVENTING THE SELF: REFRAMING YOUR BELIEFS AND REIGNITING YOUR PURPOSE

The New you, show up and recover.

Now we look into the process of reconstructing one's essence. It serves as a guide for individuals aiming to reinvent themselves, represent their newfound identity, reach their potential, and ultimately recover all aspects of their lives, as well as positively impact others. This chapter is undoubtedly essential for anyone seeking personal growth and fulfilment.

Reinvention

To start, let's explore the concept of reinvention. It is a fundamental element in the process of uncovering the true self, shedding limiting beliefs, and embracing new possibilities. Reinventing oneself requires taking a deep dive into the core values, passions, and aspirations one holds. By reframing our beliefs and challenging the preconceived notions we have about ourselves, we create the space for personal transformation.

Reinvention is a powerful concept that plays a crucial role in starting over in life. It is not just about making superficial changes; it's about a fundamental transformation of oneself. Here's how reinvention contributes to starting over:

When you decide to reinvent yourself, you consciously shed your old identity, which may have been defined by past failures, disappointments, or limiting beliefs. This shedding allows you to let go of the baggage that might have been holding you back.

Reinvention is an invitation to explore new possibilities and interests. It's a chance to redefine your goals and aspirations based on your current desires and passions. This embrace of new possibilities is essential for starting over because it opens avenues you may not have considered before.

Reinvention often involves breaking free from self-imposed limitations. It challenges you to step out of your comfort zone, confront fears, and take calculated risks. This freedom from limitations can be liberating and empowering, enabling you to move forward with confidence.

Reinventing oneself isn't always easy. It can be a journey filled with ups and downs. However, it helps build resilience as you learn to adapt, persevere, and overcome challenges. This newfound resilience becomes an asset as you navigate your fresh start in life.

Reinvention allows you to align your life with your values and principles. When your actions and choices are in harmony with your core beliefs, you experience a sense of authenticity and purpose, which is crucial for a successful new beginning.

Life often presents us with unexpected transitions, like job changes, relationship shifts, or health challenges. Reinvention equips you with the mindset and skills to adapt to these changes, turning them into opportunities for growth and renewal.

As you reinvent yourself, you embark on a journey of self-discovery. You learn more about who you are, what you're capable of, and what truly matters to you. This self-awareness is a vital foundation for starting over with clarity and intention.

Your process of reinvention can serve as an inspiration to others. By demonstrating the courage to change and grow, you become a role model for those who may be facing similar challenges or seeking to make a fresh start in life.

In essence, reinvention is not just about starting over; it's about evolving into the best version of yourself. It's a dynamic process that empowers you to create a new narrative, one that reflects your authentic self and allows you to move forward with renewed self-assurance and purpose. So, embrace the opportunity to reinvent yourself, represent the new you, and reach for the future with confidence, knowing that your journey of starting over is also a journey of growth, resilience, and transformation.

The next step in this journey is representation. Once we have embarked on the path of reinvention, it becomes crucial to showcase our newfound identity to the world. This act of representation helps to solidify the changes we have made internally and allows others to perceive and interact with the new versions of ourselves. It serves as a reminder that growth and change are not only personal endeavours but also social ones. However, representation alone is not enough. To truly reach our potential and manifest our reinvented selves, we must actively pursue our goals and dreams. This process involves setting clear intentions, taking inspired action, and persisting in the face of adversity. By embodying our new identity authentically and intentionally, we create the foundation for success and fulfilment in all aspects of our lives.

Reaching our potential is not solely for our benefit; it also enables us to positively impact others. When we fully embrace our reinvented selves and tap into our unique abilities, we become catalysts for change and inspiration. Our authenticity and unwavering pursuit of purpose create a ripple effect, inspiring those around us to embark on their own paths of self-discovery and reinvention. Ultimately, the process of reconstructing our essence is about recovery. It is about reclaiming all aspects of our lives that may have been lost, neglected, or stifled. It is a journey of healing, rediscovery, and embracing all parts of ourselves, both light and dark. Through this process, we regain our power and emerge stronger, more whole, and more aligned with our true essence.

How can individuals reinvent their sense of self?

1. Self-reflection and introspection: Take time to reflect on your current beliefs, values, strengths, weaknesses, and aspirations. Engage in activities like journaling, meditation, or therapy to gain a deeper understanding of yourself and the beliefs that may be holding you back.

2. Question your beliefs: Identify limiting beliefs or negative thought patterns that may be hindering your personal growth. Question the validity and origin of these beliefs and challenge them by seeking evidence or alternative perspectives that can help you redefine them.

3. Seek new knowledge and perspectives: Expose yourself to new ideas, knowledge, and diverse perspectives. Read books, listen to podcasts, attend workshops, or converse with people with different beliefs or life experiences. This exposure can challenge your existing beliefs and provide new insights.

4. Experiment and try new things: Step outside your comfort zone and try activities or experiences that are different from your usual routine. Engage in hobbies, explore new interests, or take up challenging projects that push your boundaries. The process of experimenting helps in discovering hidden talents or passions that can shape your renewed sense of purpose.

5. Surround yourself with positive influences: Surround yourself with people who uplift and inspire you. Engage with friends, mentors, or support groups that align with

your personal growth goals. Seek out role models who embody the qualities or values you aspire to cultivate in yourself.

6. Set goals and create a plan: Identify specific areas of personal growth or areas where you want to redefine your beliefs. Set realistic goals and create a plan to achieve them. Breaking down bigger goals into smaller, manageable steps can help in building momentum and achieving a sense of progress, reinforcing a renewed sense of purpose.

7. Embrace discomfort and learn from failures: Growth often happens outside our comfort zones, so be willing to embrace discomfort and take risks. Understand that failures and setbacks are part of the journey and offer valuable lessons. Learn from them, adapt, and persevere with resilience.

8. Practice self-compassion and gratitude: Be kind to yourself throughout this process and practice self-compassion. Embrace your vulnerability and acknowledge that personal growth is a continuous process. Additionally, cultivating gratitude can help shift your mindset towards focusing on positive aspects of your life, further empowering personal growth.

9. Take action and make changes: Ultimately, personal growth requires taking action and making changes. Whether it's adopting new habits, letting go of toxic relationships, or making bold career decisions, commit to the choices aligned with your renewed beliefs and sense of self. Remember, this process is unique to each individual, and it takes time and patience. Embrace the journey, celebrate small victories along the way, and be open to the transformations that unfold.

Reconstructing Your Essence

In the journey of beginning again, one of the most profound transformations you can undergo is the reconstruction of your essence. Your essence is the core of who you are, the sum total of your beliefs, values, and purpose. It is the foundation upon which your life is built, and sometimes, it requires a renovation.

The Power of Belief

Beliefs are the lenses through which you perceive the world. They shape your thoughts, emotions, and actions. They can either propel you forward or hold you back. In this chapter, we will explore how to examine, challenge, and reshape your beliefs to better align with your aspirations.

Examining Your Belief System

The first step in reconstructing your essence is to take a closer look at your belief system. Your beliefs have been shaped by your upbringing, experiences, and the people you've encountered along the way. Some beliefs serve you well, while others may limit your potential.

Identify Limiting Beliefs: Begin by identifying any beliefs that have been hindering your progress. These might be beliefs such as "I'm not good enough," "I can't change," or "I'm destined to fail."

Question Their Validity: Challenge the validity of these limiting beliefs. Ask yourself if there's evidence to support them or if they are simply assumptions you've held onto.

Cultivating a Growth Mindset

Central to the reconstruction of your essence is adopting a growth mindset. A growth mindset is the belief that your abilities and intelligence can be developed through effort, learning, and perseverance. With a growth mindset, you are more likely to embrace challenges, view failures as opportunities, and persist in the face of setbacks.

Expand your capabilities.

Learn from Failure: Failure is not a reflection of your worth but a stepping stone toward success. When you fail, analyse what went wrong, and use that knowledge to improve. Slow, but each step takes you closer to your destination.

Reigniting Your Purpose

Reigniting your purpose is about rediscovering what truly matters to you and aligning your beliefs and actions with that purpose. Your purpose is your guiding star, the source of motivation and meaning in your life.

Reflect on Your Passions: What are the activities and pursuits that ignite your passion? What brings you joy and fulfilment? These are often clues to your purpose.

Reconstructing your essence is a continual process. It requires self-reflection, the courage to challenge your beliefs, and the commitment to align your actions with your purpose. As you reconstruct your essence, you will find that you are not merely beginning again but evolving into a more authentic, purpose-driven, and empowered version of yourself.

In the next chapter, we will explore the importance of perspective in your journey of reinvention. Perspective is the lens through which you view the world and your own transformation, and it can profoundly impact your ability to navigate the challenges and opportunities that lie ahead.

The Importance of Perspective in Your Journey of Reinvention

In the journey of reinvention, perspective is not merely a passive viewpoint; it is the active lens through which you perceive the world and your own transformation. Your perspective shapes your thoughts, emotions, decisions, and actions. It is a powerful force that can significantly impact your ability to navigate the challenges and opportunities that lie ahead. Here's why perspective is so crucial in your journey of reinvention:

1. Clarity of Vision: Perspective provides clarity by helping you see where you've been, where you are, and where you want to go. It allows you to set meaningful goals and create a vision for your future. Without the right perspective, you may stumble blindly without a sense of direction.

2. Resilience: Life is filled with challenges and setbacks. A positive perspective enables you to bounce back from adversity. Instead of seeing obstacles as insurmountable roadblocks, you view them as opportunities for growth and learning. This resilience is crucial in the process of reinvention.

3. Adaptability: Perspective allows you to adapt to changing circumstances. When you're open to different viewpoints and ways of thinking, you're better equipped to adjust your course as needed. Flexibility is a valuable trait when starting anew.

4. Mindset Shift: The way you perceive your circumstances and challenges greatly influences your mindset. A growth-

oriented perspective fosters a belief that you can learn, improve, and overcome obstacles. A fixed mindset, on the other hand, can hinder your progress by making you resistant to change.

5. Motivation: A positive perspective can be a powerful source of motivation. When you view your goals and dreams with enthusiasm and optimism, you're more likely to stay committed to your journey, even when faced with difficulties.

6. Gratitude: Perspective allows you to appreciate what you have rather than focus on what you lack. Gratitude is a potent force that can boost your overall well-being and help you find contentment in the present moment.

7. Empathy and Connection: A broader perspective enables you to understand the experiences and feelings of others. This empathy fosters stronger relationships and a sense of belonging, which can be invaluable as you reinvent yourself with the support and understanding of those around you.

8. Learning and Growth: A growth-oriented perspective encourages continuous learning and personal development. It drives you to seek new experiences, acquire new skills, and expand your knowledge, all of which are essential components of starting afresh.

9. Overcoming Fear: Perspective can help you reframe fear and uncertainty. Instead of being paralyzed by fear, you can see it as a natural part of growth and use it as a motivator to take calculated risks and move forward.

Overcoming Fear Through Perspective

Fear is a natural and universal human emotion. It's hardwired into our brains as a survival mechanism, helping us identify and react to potential threats However, in the journey of reinvention or beginning again; fear can often become an obstacle, holding us back from taking necessary risks and seizing opportunities for growth. This is where the power of perspective comes into play.

1. Acknowledging Fear as a Natural Emotion: It's okay to feel fear when embarking on something new or uncertain. In fact, it's a sign that you're stepping out of your comfort zone, which is where growth happens.

2. Understanding the Role of Fear: Perspective allows you to understand the role of fear in your journey. Instead of seeing it as a roadblock, you can view it as a signal that you're on the verge of something important. Fear often accompanies significant opportunities, signalling that what lies ahead is meaningful and worth pursuing.

3. Embracing Fear as a Motivator: A shift in perspective enables you to use fear as a motivator. Instead of letting fear paralyze you, you can harness its energy to propel you forward. Fear can provide the adrenaline rush you need to take action and make bold decisions.

4. Calculated Risk-Taking: With the right perspective, you can differentiate between irrational fear and legitimate concerns. You can assess risks more objectively, weighing the potential benefits against the drawbacks. This enables you to take calculated risks rather than impulsive ones.

5. Viewing Failure as a Learning Opportunity: Perspective helps you reframe your relationship with failure. Instead of

fearing it, you can see failure as a natural part of growth and a valuable learning opportunity. Each failure brings lessons that can inform your future decisions and actions.

6. Fostering Resilience: A perspective that views fear as a motivator fosters resilience. It teaches you to bounce back from setbacks, knowing that fear and failure are not permanent states but temporary experiences on your journey.

7. Celebrating Courage: When you reframe fear as a motivator, you begin to celebrate courage. Taking action despite fear becomes a source of pride and empowerment. You learn that you have the strength to face challenges head-on.

8. Embracing Uncertainty: Perspective also helps you embrace uncertainty. Rather than fearing the unknown, you can see it as an opportunity for growth and exploration. Uncertainty becomes the canvas on which you can paint your reinvention.

9. Realizing Fear's Diminishing Power: Over time, as you consistently face and reframe fear, its power diminishes. You become less controlled by it and more in control of your choices. This shift is liberating and empowering.

10. Cultivating a Growth Mindset: Ultimately, the ability to reframe fear is closely linked to cultivating a growth mindset. It's the belief that you can learn, adapt, and grow from your experiences. This mindset not only helps you overcome fear but also fuels your journey of reinvention.

11. Personal Fulfilment: Ultimately, the right perspective can lead to a deeper sense of personal fulfilment. It enables you to align your actions with your values and purpose, leading to a more meaningful and satisfying life.

In summary, perspective is your lens through which you view the world and your own journey. By cultivating a positive, growth-oriented perspective, you can navigate the challenges and opportunities of reinvention with greater resilience, clarity, and motivation, ultimately leading to a more fulfilling and successful journey. It is a powerful tool that can transform your reinvention journey into a voyage of self-discovery and personal growth.

MINDSET SHIFT

May had always been known as a kind and compassionate soul, always willing to lend a helping hand to those in need. May had faced her fair share of challenges in life, but she had a secret weapon that helped her overcome them - her unwavering positive mindset.

May had experienced a major setback in her career when the company she had worked for went bankrupt. She had poured her heart and soul into that job, and the sudden loss left her feeling defeated and lost. However, May was not one to stay down for long. She knew that her mindset would be the key to her success in the journey of beginning again.

As May started her job search, she encountered rejection after rejection. The job market was tough, and many employers were looking for skills she didn't possess. But May refused to let these setbacks define her. Instead, she began to view each rejection as an opportunity to learn and grow.

She started taking online courses to acquire new skills and networked tirelessly to expand her connections. With each rejection, her determination grew stronger. She would tell herself, "I may not have the experience they're looking for now, but I can learn and improve. I am capable of anything I set my mind to."

One day, after what felt like an endless string of rejections, May received a call from a company she had applied to weeks earlier. They were impressed with her positive attitude and her willingness to learn. They offered her a position that required some training but had great potential for growth. May eagerly accepted, recognizing it as the opportunity she had been waiting for.

As May settled into her new role, her mindset became her greatest asset. She approached her work with enthusiasm and a belief that she could excel in any task put before her. She embraced challenges as opportunities to expand her knowledge and skills, just as she had during her job search.

Her colleagues soon noticed her unwavering optimism and willingness to take on new responsibilities. They admired her ability to remain composed under pressure and to find solutions to even the most complex problems. May's positive mindset was not only benefiting her but also inspiring those around her.

Over time, May's career began to soar. She took on leadership roles, mentored others, and became a respected figure in her industry. But her journey to begin again was about more than her career success. It was a testament to the power of mindset.

May had learned that setbacks and challenges were not roadblocks but stepping stones on her path to growth and success. She had shifted her perspective from one of defeat to one of resilience and opportunity. Her mindset had transformed her life, allowing her to not only survive but thrive in the face of adversity.

As May looked back on her journey, she knew that her positive mindset had been the driving force behind her success. It enabled her to reinvent herself, overcome obstacles, and achieve her dreams. May had truly begun again, and her mindset had made all the difference.

How do I know this is a wake-up call?

Identifying the storm in one's life that serves as a wake-up call to start afresh and begin again can be a deeply personal and subjective process. However, despite its uniqueness, there are some steps that may help individuals navigate this journey and find clarity in the chaos.

First and foremost, self-reflection is key. Taking the time to look inward and evaluate your current situation is essential in understanding the storm that is brewing within. Assess your emotions, thought patterns, and overall satisfaction with your life. Do you find yourself feeling overwhelmed, stuck, or consistently unhappy? These feelings can serve as powerful indicators that change is necessary.

Secondly, it's important to recognize patterns in your life. By reflecting on any recurring challenges or negative situations, you may be able to identify a common theme or trigger. This insight can provide guidance in pinpointing the storm causing distress and create an opportunity for transformation.

In addition to mental and emotional reflection, it's crucial to pay attention to the physical and emotional manifestations of the storm. Excessive stress, feelings of hopelessness, physical health issues, or strained relationships may all be signs that a storm is wreaking havoc on your life. Acknowledging these manifestations is a critical step in addressing the storm head-on.

Evaluating your life goals and values is another essential aspect of the journey toward identifying the storm in your life. Take the time to assess whether your current lifestyle aligns with your long-term aspirations and personal values. If there is a significant mismatch, it may serve as a wake-up call to start fresh and make changes that align with your authentic self.

While self-reflection is important, seeking support from loved ones can also prove invaluable. Engage in open and honest conversations with family and friends who know you well. They may offer insights or observations that can help you recognize the storm you are facing. Their perspectives can provide additional clarity and support as you navigate through tough times.

When all else fails, seeking professional help can be a wise decision. If you find it challenging to identify the storm in your life, consider seeking guidance from a therapist, counsellor, or life coach. These professionals can provide objective perspectives and offer tools to help you navigate through your circumstances. They can also guide you through the process of self-discovery, empowering you to identify and address the storm in your life.

Ultimately, trust your intuition throughout this journey. Deep down, you may already know when it is time for a fresh start. Listen to your inner voice and be open to embracing change and growth.

Finally, it is important to remember that identifying the storm in your life and starting anew is a gradual process that requires patience, self-compassion, and determination. Everyone's journey is unique, and there is no definitive formula to follow. Take the time you need to reflect and understand yourself better. Embrace the opportunity for growth and seize the chance to begin again. With resilience and perseverance, 1 you can weather the storm and emerge stronger on the other side.

CHAPTER 8:

EMERGING RESILIENT:
REPRESENTING THE NEW YOU
WHAT IS YOUR PHILOSOPHY?
- JIM ROHN

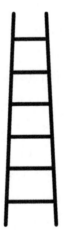

Trust the Process: A Journey of Faith and Hope

"Trust the process" is a common phrase used to encourage individuals to have faith in the journey towards achieving their goals, even if the path may be unclear or challenging at times. It acknowledges that success is rarely immediate and requires consistent effort over time.

Trusting the process involves focusing on the present moment and taking small steps towards one's goals rather than becoming overwhelmed by the result. It requires patience, perseverance, and a willingness to learn from setbacks and failures. Trusting the process can be difficult, especially when progress is not immediately visible, or obstacles arise. However, by remaining committed to the journey and having faith in the process, individuals can develop the resilience and determination needed to achieve their goals. Overall, "trusting the process" is a mindset that can help individuals stay motivated and focused on their goals, even when the path forward may be unclear or challenging. By trusting in the journey and remaining committed to their goals, individuals can ultimately achieve success and reach their full potential.

The Unexpected Turn

It was the winter of 2018 when my life took a dramatic turn. After a successful book launch, my world was suddenly disrupted by circumstances beyond my control. I found myself lost in a path I never anticipated, wondering how it all came to be. The journey ahead seemed unbearable, leaving me feeling crippled, exhausted, and filled with pain. As a parent, Hopelessness surrounded me, and I couldn't fathom how we were still standing amid it all.

The Resilience Within

"Mrs. C, can you come quickly," the voice on the other end of the line repeatedly called out. Each day, it became a familiar routine, drawing me into a world I never imagined I would be a part of. I became a constant presence, gaining access to every room, even if it was for reasons, I never wanted in the first place. I felt like I belonged there, but it was all overshadowed by shame and the strain of putting up a strong front. In truth, I was crumbling inside, shattered in pieces. The days ahead seemed bleak, and I found myself dreading the uncertainty that awaited me. I sought answers from God, only to be met with silence.

Trusting in Unseen Grace

Yet, amidst the chaos and pain, I heard a whisper from God, urging me to be still and know that He is God. His voice cut through the darkness, reminding me that His grace is sufficient and that in my weakness, He is strong. Though these words often felt unclear, I clung to them, repeating the prayer of "grace, grace, grace." Even in the loneliness that engulfed me, I learned to let go of relationships that couldn't withstand the storm and treasure those few who stayed by my side.

Faithful in Every Step

Looking back now, I can confidently say that God is faithful—faithful to guide me, faithful to carry me through every storm. Along this arduous journey, I discovered the importance of trusting in His ways, even when they made no sense to me. Despite my resistance to the path and the pain it brought, I learned that He had my best interests at heart. All I needed to do was trust the process, knowing that there is no situation that goes to waste with God. With every step, He worked things out for my good and offered hope in the most unlikely places.

Embrace the Process

So, I encourage you to trust the process alongside me. Sometimes, life takes us on detours we never wanted, but within those twists and turns lie opportunities for growth, healing, and blessings beyond our wildest imagination. God's ways are higher than our own, and though we may not always understand why certain things happen, He knows the end from the beginning. No matter what you're going through, have faith in the One who holds your future. Trust in His unwavering love and allow Him to lead you through the process with strength and hope.

Reflecting on my journey, I can wholeheartedly declare that when we trust the process, we open ourselves up to miracles, restoration, and a deeper connection with the One who has the power to turn situations around. May you find solace and inspiration in these words, and may you walk the path of trust with unwavering faith.

Unleash the giant in you.

Yes, that's correct. The phrase "Unleash the giant in you" is often used as a motivational message to encourage people to realize their full potential and overcome any obstacles that may be holding them back. By setting clear goals, developing a positive mindset, and surrounding oneself with supportive individuals, one can work towards achieving their dreams and unleashing their inner greatness. It's important to remember that success is not always easy, and setbacks are a natural part of the process, but by persevering and learning from mistakes, one can achieve their goals and reach their full potential.

Everything you want is at the end of your fears.

The statement "everything you want is at the end of your fears" suggests that the things we truly desire in life often lie beyond the obstacles and challenges that we fear the most. In other words, our fears can hold us back from achieving our goals and realizing our dreams, but by facing and overcoming those fears, we can unlock a path towards success and fulfilment.

Of course, facing your fears is easier said than done. It can be a difficult and scary process, but it is important to remember that the things we want most in life often require us to step out of our comfort zones and take risks. By confronting our fears head-on and pushing through our limitations, we can develop resilience, gain confidence, and achieve the things we once thought were impossible.

So, if you want to achieve your goals and find success, it is important to identify the fears and obstacles that are holding you back and take steps to overcome them. With persistence, determination, and a willingness to face your fears, you can unlock a path towards greater happiness and fulfilment in life.

It's also worth noting that facing your fears doesn't always mean completely overcoming them. Sometimes it is simply about acknowledging them and learning to live with them in a way that does not hold you back. It is about finding the courage to act despite your fears and not letting them dictate your decisions or limit your potential. The statement "everything you want is at the end of your fears" is a reminder that the things we desire most in life often require us to face our fears and push through our limitations. It's not always easy, but the rewards can be great, and the journey towards overcoming our fears can be a transformative and empowering experience.

The rock bottom is a set-up.

"Rock bottom" is a term commonly used to describe a state of extreme difficulty, adversity, or crisis. It's often used to refer to a point in someone's life when they feel like they've hit the lowest point possible and they're struggling to cope with the challenges they're facing. For different people, the experience of hitting rock bottom can vary widely. It may be the result of a personal crisis such as a serious illness, the loss of a loved one, addiction, financial ruin, or emotional trauma. It may involve feelings of hopelessness, despair, shame, and deep emotional pain. People who hit rock bottom may feel like they have lost control of their lives and are unable to see a way forward.

However, it is important to remember that hitting rock bottom can also be a turning point. It can be a wake-up call that prompts people to seek help, make changes in their lives, and start working towards a better future. Sometimes, the experience of hitting rock bottom can lead to a newfound sense of strength, resilience, and determination to overcome challenges and achieve goals. If you or someone you know is struggling with difficult circumstances or feeling like they have hit rock bottom, it's important to seek help and support. There are many resources available, including counselling services, support groups, and hotlines that can help and guidance during difficult times.

What are your pain points? Are you stuck?

Being stuck can be a frustrating and difficult experience and can cause a few pain points. Here are some common pain points that people may experience when they feel stuck:

Lack of progress, feelings of helplessness and hopelessness, making it difficult to find a way forward. Finding yourself in a trapped in a situation that you can't change or control. Stress and anxiety, worrying about the future and feeling uncertain about what lies ahead. Are you isolated, or lacking confidence, stuck in a negative cycle. Do you find yourself doubting your abilities and question your decisions. Overall, being stuck can be a challenging and unpleasant experience, but it's important to remember that it's possible to overcome it. By identifying the source of your problem and taking action to address it, you can regain momentum and move forward towards your goals.

Getting yourself unstuck is hard work, but necessary. In some cases, therapy may be your best option.

Therapy sets you free, it frees up your mind, it helps with your decision-making, and it's a safe place to unpack. Many people make the mistake of unpacking and trusting the wrong people with their pain or dreams. Some of our lives are marred with trauma and therapy is crucial to our healing journey.

Writing therapy helped me a lot.

On reflection when I wrote my first book. I thought I was just writing a story. I did not know that that was my way to freedom from my mind, freedom from trauma, freedom from the prison that I did not know I was in.

It was only when I was writing a certain part in the story that I broke down, I had questions that I never asked myself or anyone, but in that moment, I asked the question as I was writing. I got my answer when I broke down in tears but struggled to believe it; I struggled go past it. I sat there with my head spinning, and all I had to say to myself was all along, it was ….

I spent a few days contemplating, and eventually, went online and searched for a Christian Therapist. An extensive list came up with faces, and I was just scrolling down reading their profiles, and I settled for one lady, Janice. I picked up my phone.

Janice picked up the phone and introduced herself in a warm voice and asked if she can help me. I told her I needed help, she paused for a moment, and said it took you long today to call, Lynn. I said yes, a very long time. She said would you like us to book your time and a date? I agreed and she gave me a date that was two days after my call.

I went to see Janice along with my script. She set me in a nice calm relaxing room with a glass of water and she sat across me.

She looked at me and asked me how she could be of help. I said, I got stuck writing my script, and I broke down. Can you help me? She asked me what I was writing about, and I said my life.

She smiled at me, and she said you are already halfway there. Can I have a look at the script? Writing was the beginning of my healing journey.

Rejection Is Redirection

Tendo once applied for a highly competitive internship at a prestigious company that he had dreamed of working for. The interview process was intense, and he was confident in his qualifications and experience. However, he received the unfortunate news that he was not selected for the position.

Initially, he felt disappointed and discouraged, as he had set his heart on this opportunity. However, Tendo made a conscious decision to bounce back from rejection and view it as a chance for personal growth. Instead of dwelling on the setback, he focused on the lessons he could learn and the doors that might open as a result.

Shortly after his rejection, he came across an advertisement for a position at a smaller, lesser-known startup in the same field. Intrigued by the job description, Tendo decided to apply, seeing it as an opportunity to gain experience in a different setting. Surprisingly, He was called for an interview and was offered the position.

Working at the startup exposed me to a dynamic and fast-paced environment, where He had the chance to wear multiple hats and take on substantial responsibilities. This experience not only broadened his skill set but also allowed him to develop a strong network within the industry. Tendo discovered that he thoroughly enjoyed the startup environment and the autonomy it offered.

Additionally, during his time at the startup, He became acquainted with an individual who eventually introduced him to a mentor. This mentor guided Tendo and provided him with invaluable advice and connections that he would not have had access to otherwise. This connection ultimately led him to a different job opportunity, which turned out to be a perfect fit for his long-term career plans.

Looking back, if Tendo had been accepted for the internship at the prestigious company, He would have missed out on the valuable experiences, connections, and personal growth that he gained through the rejection. It taught Tendo the importance of resilience and embracing unexpected opportunities, ultimately redirecting his path in a positive way.

This experience reinforced the notion that rejection is not always a setback but rather a chance to explore new avenues and discover unforeseen opportunities that can shape our lives in ways we may never have expected.

Redeem

Life is full of challenges, but whatever you do try to pick yourself up, feel the gap with new energy, affirmations, embrace you, acknowledge you and the imperfect you, contact the inner you, exchange the emotions, keep the good, and redeem the time.

"Redeeming the time" is a phrase that means making the most of the time that you have and using it wisely and productively. It's about being mindful of how you spend your time and making sure that you prioritize the things that are important to you. The idea of redeeming the time has been around for centuries and is often associated with the Christian faith. In the Bible, the apostle Paul encourages his followers to "redeem the time" in several of his letters, urging them to use their time wisely and make the most of every opportunity.

In a broader sense, however, the concept of redeeming the time can apply to anyone, regardless of their religious beliefs. It's about recognizing the value of time and being intentional about how you use it, whether that's by pursuing your goals, spending time with loved ones, or engaging in activities that bring you fulfilment and joy.

Yes, that is correct. Redeeming the time is about making the most of the time you have and being intentional about how you use it. It's important to prioritize the things that matter most to you and to use your time in a way that aligns with your values and goals. By being mindful of how you spend your time and making the most of every opportunity, you can live a more fulfilling and productive life.

When it comes to beginning again in life, time management is key. The need to set priorities, creating schedules and allocating time to different activities based on their importance and urgency. Self-discipline, focus, and willingness to work on more important tasks helps to get a desired outcome.

By managing your time effectively, you can increase your productivity, reduce stress, and achieve your goals more efficiently.

And so, Tendo, now a man on a mission continued his journey maximizing his day and rewriting his life. He had discovered a powerful strategy that would forever change the way he approached his work and daily responsibilities. He had heard about the 20% productivity rule and was determined to apply it to his life. This rule stated that if he focused on the most important tasks, he could get 80% of the results in just 20% of his time. It sounded too good to be true, but Tendo was eager to put it to the test.

He woke up early, feeling energized and excited for the day ahead. He knew that setting goals was key, so he sat down with a cup of coffee and a notepad. Tendo wrote down three main goals for the day: finish a report for work, revise his novel, and spend quality time with his family. These goals were achievable but would require focus and dedication.

Tendo knew that prioritizing tasks was essential, so he analysed his goals and identified the most urgent and important tasks. He realized that the work report was due in two days, so he decided to tackle that one first. He created a schedule, allocating two hours of uninterrupted time to work on the report. With a clear plan in mind, Tendo felt confident and ready to tackle the day.

As Tendo sat down to start his work, he realized that distractions could easily derail his progress. So, he made a conscious effort to eliminate them. He turned off his phone, closed all social media tabs, and put a sign on his office door indicating that he was busy and should not be disturbed. Tendo knew that to maximize his day, he needed to stay focused and avoid unnecessary distractions.

After a couple of hours of concentrated work, Tendo felt the need to take a break. He had been advised to do so, to refresh his mind and prevent burnout. He decided to go for a short walk outside, breathing in the fresh air and allowing his thoughts to wander. This break reinvigorated him, and he returned to his office with renewed energy.

Tendo knew that to maximize his day, he needed to take care of his physical and mental health. He made sure to eat a healthy lunch, drink plenty of water, and do a quick workout session during his break. These little acts of self-care made a big difference in his overall productivity and well-being.

As the day progressed, Tendo found himself feeling overwhelmed with tasks. He realized that he could delegate some of them to others, freeing up more time for the important ones. He asked his colleague for help with a small part of the report and enlisted his wife's assistance in preparing dinner. Tendo understood the importance of teamwork and knew that by delegating tasks, he could focus on what truly mattered.

By the end of the day, Tendo had achieved all his goals. He had completed the work report, made significant revisions to his novel, and had a wonderful evening with his family. Tendo couldn't believe how much he had accomplished in just one day.

The 20% productivity rule had truly transformed his life. Tendo had learned that by setting clear goals, prioritizing tasks, creating a schedule, eliminating distractions, taking breaks, staying healthy, and delegating tasks, he could maximize his day and achieve incredible results.

Tendo went to bed that night with a sense of fulfilment and excitement for what the next day would bring. He knew that by consistently applying the 20% productivity rule, he would continue to make the most of his time and achieve his goals.

With determination and the 20% productivity rule as his guide, Tendo knew that anything was possible.

Managing personal change

Managing personal change can be a challenging process, but there are certain steps that can be taken to make it easier. It is a process, and achieving your goals may take time and effort. But with the right mindset and strategy, you can successfully manage personal change and reach your desired outcomes.

Reviving your body and spirit is essential and involves taking care of yourself both physically and mentally. Your spirit, also referred to as your inner self, essence, or soul, is the non-physical part of your being that gives you a sense of purpose, meaning, and connectedness to something greater than yourself. While your physical body is important for your survival and functioning in the world, your spirit is what gives your life depth and richness.

Having a healthy spirit can help you in providing a sense of purpose helping you to stay motivated and focused on your goals.

A healthy spirit promotes emotional stability. It can help you feel more positive, resilient, and emotionally balanced. It can also help you cope with challenges and setbacks more effectively.

Thirdly when you are connected to your spirit, you are more l compassionate and extend empathy towards others. This, however, enables you to build stronger and more meaningful relationships.

In summary, your spirit matters because it is an integral part of your overall well-being and can influence your physical, emotional, and social wellbeing. Nurturing your spirit can help you live a more fulfilling and meaningful life.

Having a good night sleep, eating health, regular exercising, self-care, quality time with meaning relations, being fully present and engaged and practicing gratitude.

By taking care of your body and mind, you can revive your spirit and feel more energized and motivated to tackle the challenges of daily life.

The art of resilience – change the narrative.

Closed doors mean preparation.

Dancing in the wilderness – find your song, encourage yourself, be intentional about laughter, rest, take each day as it comes.

Rejection is Redirection - build resilience, sharpen your senses, it is your time to heal, focus on you first before you move on, balance yourself, choose you, as soon as you sense the vibes don't delay, act quickly, the longer you are exposed to rejection, the greater are the wounds and the longer it takes to heal, the more the negative memories, run for your life.

Stop the business of thinking the rejectors will change and keep holding on to them. If ever they are going to change, make sure they meet you again at a new level; you would have grown and developed yourself, not waiting around. Think of yourself and care for yourself, add value to yourself. This helps you to avoid unnecessary pain, especially when the rejectors decide not to accept you, or rather they accept you, but you will be a doormat and always having a feeling that you don't fully belong here.

Isolation means look within and draw strength from there – an opportunity to evaluate your life with no distractions Isolation is your gateway to coming out of the shadows and finding your true self.

When they leave, its doors opening for the new. It's an opportunity to self-reflect and grow. Don't chase after what's leaving you. If it's meant for you, it will gravitate back to you at the right time.

Renewing your mind means doing the inner work; fix the inside before the outside, don't judge the outside before you do the inner work; look intently, and look beneath the surface.

Your Identity is key.

Who Are You?

In the journey of self-discovery, the first question you must confront is, "Who are you?" It's a question that goes beyond your name and appearance. It delves into the core of your being, your values, your beliefs, and your unique essence. Take the time to introspect and define your identity.

Why Are You Here?

Life's purpose is a powerful driving force. Why are you here on this planet? What is your mission, your calling? Your purpose is like a compass guiding you through the maze of existence. It's not always easy to discern, but once you find it, your path becomes clearer.

Whose Are You?

We are interconnected beings, part of a vast web of relationships. Whose are you in this world? Who do you belong to? This question encompasses your family, your community, your affiliations, and your allegiances. Understanding where you fit in the grand scheme of things is essential for your growth.

Where Are You?

Location matters, not just in a geographical sense, but in the context of your life's journey. Where are you emotionally, spiritually, and mentally? Are you in a place of growth, stagnation, or regression? Assess your current position to determine where you need to go next.

What Are You Doing About It?

Knowing your identity, purpose, affiliations, and location is only the beginning. What actions are you taking to align with your true self? Your choices and deeds define you as much as your thoughts and beliefs. Make a conscious effort to live in accordance with your authentic self.

Which Way or Side Are You Taking?

Life is full of choices, and each choice steers you down a particular path. Are you choosing the path that aligns with your identity and purpose, or are you drifting aimlessly? Make deliberate choices that lead you toward your goals and values.

Beauty for ashes

May was known for her radiant spirit and kind heart. She had a smile that could brighten even the darkest of days and a heart that overflowed with love for her community.

However, May's life had not always been filled with sunshine. She had faced her fair share of hardships. As a child, she had lost her parents in a tragic accident, leaving her an orphan. She had grown up in the care of her elderly grandmother, Eliza, who had taught her the importance of resilience and faith.

May and her grandmother lived in a modest cottage on the outskirts of the village. Despite their simple life, they were content. Eliza would often tell May stories of her parents and share wisdom about finding beauty amid ashes. She spoke of believing in God, importance of kindness, generosity, and the power of love to heal even the deepest wounds.

One fateful evening, a terrible fire swept through their village, leaving many homes reduced to ashes. May and Eliza watched in horror as their beloved cottage was consumed by the flames. They lost all their possessions, including cherished memories of May's parents.

Devastated but not defeated, May and Eliza found shelter with a kind-hearted neighbour, Mrs. Henda, who offered them a place to stay. The village rallied together to help the fire victims, and May, with her natural ability to bring people together, organized a relief effort to assist those who had lost their homes.

Weeks turned into months, and May's resilience shone brighter than ever. She had become a pillar of strength in the village, inspiring others with her unwavering spirit. Despite the ashes that surrounded her, May continued to sow seeds of hope and love in her community.

One day, as May was helping to rebuild homes for the villagers, she stumbled upon a small, charred box buried in the ashes of her old cottage. With trembling hands, she carefully opened it. Inside, she found a collection of letters and photographs, memories of her parents that she had thought were lost forever.

Tears of joy streamed down her face as she shared the discovery with Eliza and the village. It was a symbol of hope and a reminder that beauty could indeed emerge from the ashes of despair. The love that had once filled their cottage was alive in May's heart, and it radiated out to everyone she touched.

Over time, the village was rebuilt, stronger and more tightly knit than ever before. May continued to be a source of inspiration, her smile and unwavering faith a beacon of light for all. The lessons she had learned from Eliza about finding beauty in ashes had become a living testament to the power of love, resilience, and community.

And so, in the heart of that little village, the story of May and her grandmother, Eliza, became a legend—a tale of beauty emerging from the ashes and a testament to the enduring power of the human spirit. May's life was a living example of the transformation that could occur when one had the courage to embrace life's challenges with love and unwavering faith.

Embrace your imperfections and past mistakes. They are the ashes from which the beauty of your future can emerge. Declare your identity boldly, without fear or hesitation.

Perspective is crucial in your journey of beginning again. Having the right perspective provides clarity about where you want to go and what you want to achieve in your fresh start. It helps you set clear goals and make informed decisions.

Perspective offers several benefits:

1. Clarity of Direction: A proper perspective provides clarity about your desired destination and goals, helping you make informed decisions.

2. Positive Mindset: Perspective shapes your mindset, and a positive perspective fuels optimism, resilience, and the belief that you can overcome challenges. It allows you to see opportunities in setbacks.

3. Resilience: The right perspective enables you to bounce back from setbacks, failures, and adversity, seeing them as opportunities for growth rather than insurmountable obstacles.

4. Motivation: Your perspective affects your motivation. A positive perspective keeps you motivated and committed to your goals, even in the face of obstacles or setbacks.

5. Adaptability: Life rarely goes as planned, but a flexible perspective allows you to adapt to changing circumstances and make necessary adjustments to your goals and plans.

6. Emotional Well-being: Your perspective significantly impacts your emotional well-being. Having a healthy perspective reduces stress, anxiety, and depression, promoting mental and emotional health.

7. Problem-Solving: A clear and balanced perspective helps you approach problems with a rational and creative mindset. It allows you to see multiple sides of an issue and find innovative solutions.

8. Improved Relationships: Perspective plays a vital role in your relationships by helping you understand others' viewpoints, fostering empathy, and promoting effective communication.

9. Growth and Learning: An open and growth-oriented perspective encourages continuous learning and personal development. It enables you to embrace change and new experiences as opportunities for growth.

10. Gratitude and Contentment: The right perspective helps you appreciate the present moment and find contentment in your journey. Gratitude is a powerful mindset that can transform your life. Choose to be thankful for the blessings and challenges alike. Gratitude shifts your perspective and opens your heart to the abundance that surrounds you.

Reset Your Timeline

Don't be bound by the past. Reset your timeline and create a new path that aligns with your purpose and values. Make amends where needed. Restitution is not only about repairing relationships with others but also with yourself. Your thoughts shape your reality. Renew your mind by challenging negative beliefs and embracing a positive and growth-oriented mindset. While the mind is a powerful tool for envisioning your goals, remember that action is essential. Combine your thoughts with deliberate steps toward your aspirations. A renewed mind brings numerous benefits, including improved mental health, better decision-making, increased creativity, enhanced relationships, improved physical health, greater self-awareness, improved focus and productivity, and a greater sense of purpose and meaning.

Beginning again requires you to identify negative thought patterns, challenging those beliefs, and replacing them with positive ones. It also includes practicing mindfulness, self-compassion, and cultivating a growth mindset. Surrounding yourself with positivity, engaging in self-care, seeking support, and practicing gratitude are integral parts of the journey.

While the idea of rewiring the brain may be oversimplified, neuroplasticity allows for change and adaptation over time. Aim to develop new skills and overcome challenges. Remember that your brain is unique, and the extent of change depends on several factors.

Restore what was lost Begin Again

Never look down upon yourself and never eliminate yourself from proverbs 31 because sometimes, it sounds or how we have had it being shared to us sounded more like something that is beyond us, but it's not. Take it and apply it to where you are in the same manner that I've been chained to breaking it down for you when it comes to advocating for the poor. When you go and stand up and speak for your children at school, that is advocating for them because at that point, there are voiceless; you are their voice or choose to stand up for other children you can see there's another poor kid in your child's class.

You can be all God designed you to be in whatever stage of your life, everything that happens to you; that has happened, that is happening, that will happen, it all fits in together to shape you to be the best version of yourself. All you need is to identify who you are and bring all these things together and begin again, this time is taking all these things that was meant to put you down that was meant to destroy you and putting into purpose that is clear thank you.

The phrase "What the mind can conceive, it can have" suggests that if you can imagine or visualize something in your mind, you have the power to make it a reality. While this may be true in some cases, it is not a guarantee that you can achieve everything you conceive in your mind.

The human mind is a powerful tool that can create ideas and solutions to problems, but there are often limitations to what we can achieve based on factors such as resources, time, and physical limitations. Additionally, some goals may be unrealistic or impossible to achieve, regardless of how much we conceive of them in our minds.

However, having a positive mindset and belief in oneself can be important for achieving personal goals and success. By visualizing and focusing on what you want to achieve, you can develop a clearer sense of direction and motivation to work towards your goals. It's important to remember, though, that hard work, perseverance, and a willingness to learn and adapt are also essential components of achieving success.

Benefits of a renewed mind

Renewing your mind can have many benefits, both for your mental and physical health, as well as for your overall well-being. Here are some of the potential benefits of a renewed mind:

1. Improved mental health: Renewing your mind can help reduce stress, anxiety, and depression and improve your overall mental health.

2. Better decision-making: A renewed mind helps you think more clearly and rationally, allowing you to make better decisions in all areas of your life.

3. Increased creativity: A renewed mind can help you tap into your creativity and come up with new ideas and perspectives.

4. Greater resilience: When your mind is renewed, you are better able to bounce back from setbacks and challenges and 4 maintain a positive outlook.

5. Enhanced relationships: A renewed mind can help you communicate more effectively and relate to others more positively, leading to stronger, more fulfilling relationships.

6. Improved physical health: Renewing your mind can help reduce stress and anxiety, which can, in turn, have a positive impact on your physical health, including reducing inflammation and improving immune function.

7. Spiritual growth: Renewing your mind can help deepen your spiritual life and relationship with God if that is important to you.

Overall, renewing your mind can have a profound impact on your life, improving your mental and physical health, relationships, and overall well-being.

8. Increased self-awareness: Renewing your mind involves becoming more aware of your thoughts, emotions, and behaviours, which can help you identify areas for growth and personal development.

9. Improved focus and productivity: A renewed mind can help you stay focused on your goals and tasks, allowing you to be more productive and efficient.

10. Greater sense of purpose and meaning: Renewing your mind can help you clarify your values and priorities and connect with a sense of purpose and meaning in your life.

11. Increased resilience to addiction: A renewed mind can help you develop the mental strength and resilience needed to overcome addictive behaviours and habits.

Overall, renewing your mind can have a profound impact on your life, improving your mental and physical health, relationships, productivity, and overall sense of well-being. Steps to mind renewal

Mind renewal is the process of changing the way you think about yourself, others, and the world around you. It involves letting go of old thought patterns that hold you back and adopting new beliefs that empower you to live a happier and more fulfilling life. Here are some steps to help you renew your mind:

1. Identify negative thought patterns: The first step in renewing your mind is to identify the negative thought patterns that are holding you back. These may include beliefs about yourself, others, or the world that are limiting your potential and preventing you from achieving your goals.

2. Challenge negative beliefs: Once you have identified your negative thought patterns, it's important to challenge them. Ask yourself if they are really true and look for evidence that contradicts them. This will help you to see things in a new and more positive light.

3. Replace negative thoughts with positive ones: Once you have challenged your negative beliefs, it's time to replace them with positive ones. This may involve affirmations or

positive self-talk or simply focusing on the positive aspects of a situation rather than the negative.

Have positive thoughts. This involves consciously choosing to focus on positive thoughts and beliefs about yourself, others, and the world around you. This can be done through daily affirmations, positive self-talk, and visualization exercises.

4. Practice mindfulness: Mindfulness is the practice of paying attention to the present moment without judgment. It can help you to become more aware of your thoughts and feelings and to develop a more positive and accepting attitude towards yourself and others.

5. Surround yourself with positivity: Finally, it's important to surround yourself with positive people and experiences. Seek out friendships and relationships that support and encourage you and engage in activities that bring you joy and fulfilment.

Remember that mind renewal is a process that takes time and effort. Be patient with yourself and celebrate your progress along the way.

With practice and perseverance, you can create a more positive and fulfilling life for yourself.

4. Practice gratitude: Gratitude is the practice of focusing on the positive aspects of your life and being thankful for them. By practicing gratitude on a regular basis, you can shift your focus away from negative thoughts and towards the good things in your life. This can help you to feel more positive and optimistic about your future.

5. Engage in self-care: Taking care of yourself physically, emotionally, and mentally is an important part of mind renewal. This can include things like getting enough sleep, eating a healthy diet, exercising regularly, and practicing relaxation techniques like meditation or yoga.

6. Seek support: Finally, it's important to seek support from others as you work on renewing your mind. This can include talking to a trusted friend or family member, seeking out a therapist or counsellor, or joining a support group. Having others to talk to and share your experiences with can be incredibly helpful in staying motivated and on track with your mind renewal goals.

   Remember, mind renewal is a journey, and it takes time and effort to make lasting changes. But by taking these steps and staying committed to your goals, you can create a more positive and fulfilling life for yourself.

   Have positive thoughts. This involves consciously choosing to focus on positive thoughts and beliefs about yourself, others, and the world around you. This can be done through daily affirmations, positive self-talk, and visualization exercises.

7. Practice self-compassion: Self-compassion is the practice of treating yourself with kindness, understanding, and acceptance. This means recognizing and accepting your flaws and mistakes and treating yourself with the same kindness and compassion that you would offer to a friend. By practicing self-compassion, you can reduce self-criticism and increase self-esteem.

8. Cultivate a growth mindset: A growth mindset is the belief that your abilities and intelligence can be developed through hard work, practice, and perseverance. This means embracing challenges and setbacks as opportunities for growth and learning rather than as evidence of your limitations. By cultivating a growth mindset, you can become more resilient and adaptable in the face of challenges.

9. Engage in positive activities: Engaging in positive activities that bring you joy, and fulfilment can be a powerful way to renew your mind.

This can include things like spending time with loved ones, pursuing hobbies and interests, volunteering, or engaging in creative activities like art or music.

Remember, mind renewal is a process that takes time and effort, but it can be incredibly rewarding. By taking these steps and staying committed to your goals, you can create a more positive and fulfilling life for yourself.

Finally, it's important to note that maintaining social connections and staying engaged in meaningful activities can also have a positive impact on brain function and overall well-being. Engaging in social activities and pursuing hobbies and interests can help keep the brain active and stimulated, which can help improve cognitive function over time.

In summary, while "rewiring" the brain may not be entirely accurate, there are various techniques and activities that can help individuals improve their cognitive abilities and enhance their overall brain function. Adopting a healthy lifestyle, engaging in mental and physical exercises, and staying socially and mentally active can all contribute to optimal brain performance.

CHAPTER 9:

TRANSFORMATIONAL SHIFT: REWRITING YOUR NARRATIVE AND REGAINING SELF-ASSURANCE

Regain your confidence.

As you've journeyed through the pages of this book, you've explored various facets of self-discovery, resilience, and personal growth. Now, we delve into a pivotal concept that underpins the entire process of beginning again: the transformational shift. Here, we'll explore the art of rewriting your narrative and regaining self-assurance, ultimately setting the stage for a brighter, more fulfilling future.

The Power of Your Personal Narrative

Every one of us carries a personal narrative—a story we tell ourselves about who we are, where we've come from, and what we're capable of achieving. This narrative is not set in stone; rather, it's a dynamic and evolving script that can be rewritten at any moment. Your past experiences, successes, failures, and the stories you've absorbed from others have contributed to the narrative you currently hold.

Exercise 1: Mapping Your Narrative

Take a moment to reflect on the narrative that has defined your life so far.

What are the key themes, characters, and defining moments that have emerged?

Identify which parts of your narrative empower and inspire you and which parts hold you back or limit your potential.

Recognizing the Need for Transformation

In the previous chapters, we discussed the importance of self-awareness and resilience. Now, armed with these tools, you are better equipped to recognize when your current narrative is no longer serving you. Signs that a transformational shift may be necessary include:

Persistent feelings of self-doubt and insecurity

Repeating negative patterns in your life

A sense of stagnation or unfulfillment

A growing desire for change and personal growth

The Process of Rewriting Your Narrative

Reflect on Your Values and Beliefs: To begin rewriting your narrative, start by identifying your core values and beliefs. What matters most to you in life? What principles do you want to guide your decisions and actions? Your new narrative should align with these values.

Limiting Beliefs: We all carry limiting beliefs that stem from past experiences or external influences. These beliefs often hold us back. Identify these beliefs and ask yourself if they are based on reality or outdated assumptions. Challenge and replace them with more empowering beliefs.

Set Clear Intentions: Define your goals and aspirations. Where do you want to go from here? Setting clear intentions gives your narrative a direction and purpose. It provides you with a roadmap for personal growth.

Cultivate Self-Compassion: The process of rewriting your narrative can be challenging, and setbacks may occur. Cultivate self-compassion by treating yourself with kindness and understanding, just as you would a close friend.

Seek Support: Don't embark on this journey alone. Seek out mentors, coaches, or friends who can provide guidance, encouragement, and accountability as you rewrite your narrative.

Take Inspired Action: Your new narrative will remain a story unless you take action. Break down your goals into small, manageable steps and consistently take inspired action toward them.

Regaining Self-Assurance

As you rewrite your narrative and take steps toward personal growth, your self-assurance will naturally grow. However, it's essential to remember that self-assurance is not about being perfect or never experiencing self-doubt. Instead, it's about having confidence in your ability to navigate life's challenges and learn from your experiences.

Exercise 2: The Power of Journaling

Each day, write down one thing you did that made you feel proud or confident.

Reflect on these moments and acknowledge your progress regularly.

Embracing the Journey

The process of transformation and rewriting your narrative is a journey, not a destination. Embrace the ups and downs and understand that setbacks are an integral part of growth. As you continue this path, remember that you have the power to shape your own story, redefine your narrative, and regain self-assurance. The journey of beginning again is a testament to your resilience and capacity for personal transformation.

In the final chapter of "Begin Again," we'll explore the concept of legacy and how your journey can inspire and impact others. But for now, let the transformational shift empower you to craft a narrative that reflects your true potential and leads you toward a more fulfilling life.

Regenerated May

The room was dimly lit, with the gentle glow of candles casting soft, flickering shadows on the walls. May sat in her favourite armchair, a well-worn book in one hand and a steaming cup of herbal tea in the other. She had come a long way since the beginning of her journey, and as she turned the pages of her life, she couldn't help but feel a sense of accomplishment.

In the previous chapters of "Begin Again," we explored the ups and downs of May's life, from the challenges of her past to the newfound clarity and purpose she had discovered. Now, we will explore the pivotal moment in May's life when she underwent a transformational shift. This shift allowed her to rewrite her narrative and regain self-assurance, leading her to a more fulfilled and empowered life.

The Power of Self-Reflection

May had learned the invaluable skill of self-reflection on her journey. During moments of quiet contemplation, she began to understand the patterns and beliefs that had held her back for so long. She realized that to rewrite her narrative and regain her self-assurance, she had to confront her past and insecurities head-on.

Self-reflection became her compass, guiding her towards a deeper understanding of herself. She started journaling, jotting down her thoughts, fears, and dreams. Through this process, she uncovered the stories she had been telling herself – stories that no longer served her.

These stories were like anchors, weighing her down and preventing her from moving forward.

Embracing Change

Once May had identified the stories that were holding her back, she was faced with a choice: to continue living by those old narratives or to embrace change and rewrite her story. She chose the latter. It wasn't an easy decision, and it came with its fair share of challenges, but May knew it was the only way to regain her self-assurance.

To embrace change, May started by setting clear intentions for her life. She visualized the person she wanted to become and the life she wanted to lead. This newfound clarity allowed her to make decisions that were aligned with her true self rather than being influenced by external expectations or her past.

The Power of Resilience

As May embarked on her journey of transformation, she encountered setbacks and obstacles. There were moments when self-doubt crept in, and she questioned whether she was on the right path. But she had developed a newfound resilience that allowed her to persevere. May learned that setbacks were not failures but opportunities for growth. Each challenge she faced became a stepping stone towards her transformation. She sought support from a therapist and surrounded herself with a community of like-minded individuals who uplifted and encouraged her. This support system was instrumental in helping her regain her self-assurance.

Cultivating Self-Compassion

Rewriting her narrative also involved cultivating self-compassion. May had spent years being her own harshest critic, but she now understood the importance of treating herself with kindness and understanding. She learned to forgive herself for past mistakes and to let go of the need for perfection.

Self-compassion became the foundation of her self-assurance. It allowed her to accept herself as she was, flaws and all, and to recognize her worthiness of love and success.

The Journey Continues

As May continued reflecting on her journey of transformation, she realized that it was an ongoing process. Life would continue to present challenges and opportunities for growth. But now, armed with self-reflection, a willingness to embrace change, resilience, and self-compassion, she felt more equipped than ever to face whatever came her way.

In this chapter, we've explored May's transformational shift – the moment when she decided to rewrite her narrative and regain her self-assurance. It serves as a reminder that we all have the power to change our stories, to embrace our true selves, and to live a life that is authentic and fulfilling. As you embark on your own journey of transformation, remember that it is never too late to begin again.

In the next chapter of "Begin Again," we explore the importance of cultivating gratitude and finding meaning in everyday life. Stay tuned as May's journey continues to unfold, inspiring us all to live with purpose and passion.

Overall, beginning again can be a positive and necessary step in life, as it allows for growth, change, and the pursuit of new opportunities. However, without consistency and discipline, the journey may be coupled with frustration and several reasons to give up.

The power of consistency and discipline

Consistency and discipline played crucial roles in May's transformational shift of rewriting her narrative and regaining self-assurance as she started afresh in life. Let's explore how these traits contributed to her journey:

1. Establishing New Habits: May realized that to create lasting change, she needed to develop new habits and routines that aligned with her desired narrative. She committed to consistently practicing self-care, setting time aside for meditation, exercise, and healthy eating. By consistently engaging in these habits, she started to see positive shifts in her mindset and overall well-being.

2. Setting Clear Goals: May understood the importance of setting clear, specific goals that would guide her on her path of transformation. She broke down her larger aspirations into smaller, manageable steps and created a roadmap for herself. With discipline, she committed to taking consistent action towards these goals, no matter how small the steps were.

3. Overcoming Resistance: Along her journey, May encountered resistance and obstacles that could have deterred her. However, she understood that consistent effort and discipline were key to pushing through these

challenges. She embraced discomfort and faced her fears head-on, knowing that only by consistently pushing beyond her comfort zone could she make progress.

4. Maintaining Accountability: May recognized the power of accountability in staying committed to her transformation. She sought out mentors, coaches, and like-minded individuals who held her accountable for her goals and provided support. Through regular check-ins, she stayed on track and celebrated her progress, further motivating herself to stay consistent.

5. Adapting and Learning: Consistency and discipline helped May develop a growth mindset, enabling her to adapt and learn from her experiences. She understood that change was a continuous process requiring flexibility and openness. By consistently reflecting on her journey, learning from her setbacks, and adjusting her approach, she was able to pivot when needed and continue moving forward.

6. Cultivating Patience: May recognized that transformation and rewriting her narrative took time and patience. She didn't expect instant results and understood that consistent effort over an extended period was required. With discipline, she embraced the journey, trusting in the process and believing in herself, even during challenging times.

By embodying consistency and discipline, May propelled herself forward on her path of transformation. These traits allowed her to establish new empowering habits, overcome obstacles, maintain accountability, and adapt as needed. They were the pillars that supported her in rewriting her narrative and regaining self-assurance, ultimately leading to a more fulfilling and authentic life.

Consistency and discipline are major keys to success in many areas of life, including personal development, career advancement, and achieving goals. Consistency involves regularly performing positive habits, while discipline involves the determination to avoid distractions or temptations that could interfere with reaching goals. Both of these qualities take dedication and effort, but they can lead to big accomplishments and personal growth over time.

When you remain committed to performing positive habits and behaviours consistently, you become a role model for others to follow, and you empower yourself to reach your goals. By avoiding distractions or temptations that could interfere with your long-term progress and keeping focused on the end goal, you can accomplish significant accomplishments and personal growth over time.

Consistency and discipline require commitment, effort, and patience, but they can lead to significant accomplishments and fulfilment in various areas of life.

Why is it difficult to be consistent and disciplined? Sometimes, it can be incredibly difficult to stick to a routine and maintain discipline in our lives.

While we may want to stay consistent and follow through on our goals, human nature, temptations, distractions, fear of failure, and lack of accountability can make this an incredibly challenging endeavour. We must fight against our own natural tendencies, battle the many distractions of modern life, stay motivated when things get tough, push past our fear of failure, and hold ourselves accountable for our actions. It won't be easy – but with self-awareness, determination, and support from others, we can persevere and eventually gain the consistency and discipline needed to reach our full potential.

Your transformational shift requires your will, mental being, emotional, spiritual, social, and financial being. The choices you make matters and has an impact on your transformational shift.

CHOICES.

Spiritual wellbeing

In the bible in Mathew 25:31 - 46 it's a glimpse of the choices we can make in life to be more like Christ and how our choices can make a difference in our lives and that of others. One of the key choices one can make is to connect with God. The shift in your life requires you to have strength from a higher power and strength within you.

Today, I want to talk to you about choices that can help us to be fully connected in Christ and making a difference in our lives and our surroundings. The beauty of Christ is that He gives us a choice daily regardless of the circumstances surrounding us. There is freedom in Christ, and there is liberty.

Salvation is Choice

We are given an invitation to follow him, and we have a choice to follow Christ, and it's never imposed on us. God is very patient, compassionate, and loving. He gives us a choice to leave the old and embrace the new that is in Christ Jesus. Having a new identity that reflects the nature of God and enables us to see, feel, hear, and respond to the cries around us.

When we choose to follow Christ, He sets us free and guides us. Galatians 5:1 - 22 is available to us the fruit of the Spirit is love, joy, peace, forbearance, kindness, goodness, faithfulness, gentleness, and self-control. If we walk in God's nature and exhibit the spirit of love, kindness, goodness, forgiveness, and giving to ourselves and others become easier. Galatians 5:1, "It is for freedom that Christ has set us free. Stand firm, then, and do not let yourselves be burdened again by a yoke of slavery."

As I reflect on what freedom means to me now and how I express it in my daily life, I realized I have a responsibility to decide each day, whether I am aware of it or not, how I will go about life today and allow Christ to be at the centre of it. What I do with my time, resources, words, thoughts, and actions are all choices I will make, but one thing I am certain of is if I walk in the freedom that Christ gave me, I can accomplish more than I could imagine.

Each day, we are presented with an opportunity to make choices; to decide what to do, what to think, and what to say. We can bring life or death to any situation. We are entrusted with that responsibility from the beginning. In Genesis, man was given dominion over the earth. Man was given the responsibility to decide how to make it better or worse. This begins in each of our hearts. We can choose to love unconditionally, or we can be like what the scripture says in Proverbs 23:7: 'for he is like one who is inwardly calculating.

"Eat and drink!" he says to you, but his heart is not with you' (ESV). We can be true to ourselves and true to our call, or we can live a life of pretence. I would like to pose some questions to you:

What's in your heart?

What are you saying?

What are you tearing down or building each day of your life?

Proverbs 4:23 says, 'keep your heart with all vigilance, for from it flow the springs of life' (ESV). It is not easy to keep our hearts pure, and alone we cannot do it, but when we choose to live our lives as an offering to the Lord, then through us, He can make the necessary changes in our lives and in the lives of others.

2. Forgiveness is choice.

Jesus gives us the choice to forgive, others and in some cases, we must make a choice to forgive ourselves to be all he created us to be. I have faced a lot of rejection in my life and have endured a lot of pain too and to the point when I didn't know who I was anymore.

There were so many times I wanted to or could have cut ties and never looked back. But God orchestrates our lives. The choice to love despite all, is the best way we can present Christ in our lives to others.

There was a time in my life when I questioned some relationships, where I felt I had poured out so much but was feeling like it was a one-sided relationship. I was on the brink of walking away or even treating them the way they were treating me.

However, God's word causes us to have a different perspective. It draws us back to love despite all and reminds us that we don't do things for man to uphold us, but we do it unto the Living God who sees and knows all that is in the heart of man.

Again, the choice to love benefits us more than the one who has wronged us. Paul wrote, 'But I will rejoice even if I lose my life, pouring it out like a liquid offering to God...' Philippians 2:17 (NLT).

When we know and feel His love, it changes our perspective of life and helps us embrace others more easily. Unless we have known this kind of love, it is hard to walk fully in God's plan and purpose for our lives. Christ died for us and showed us this kind of love first.

Emotional and Mental Well-Being

Choices play a significant role in May's transformational shift, as they directly impact her emotional and mental well-being. Let's dive into why choices matter in her journey of rewriting her narrative:

1. Empowerment and Ownership: May recognizes that the choices she makes shape her life and well-being. By taking ownership of her decisions, she embraces the power to create change. This sense of empowerment sparks the motivation needed to prioritize her emotional and mental well-being.

2. Aligning with Core Values: May understands the importance of aligning her choices with her core values. Making choices that reflect her true desires and beliefs allows her to live authentically, cultivates a sense of inner peace and fulfilment and strengthens her self-assurance.

3. Cultivating Growth Mindset: May's choice to embrace a growth mindset significantly contributes to her emotional and mental well-being. Instead of succumbing to fear or self-doubt, she chooses to view challenges as opportunities for growth and learning. This mindset shift helps her bounce back from setbacks, maintain a positive outlook, and increase resilience.

4. Establishing Healthy Boundaries: May understands that setting boundaries is crucial for her emotional and mental well-being. She consciously chooses to establish boundaries

in relationships and work-life balance, saying no to activities or people that drain her energy or compromise her self-worth. By making these choices, she protects her emotional well-being and maintains a healthy sense of self-assurance.

5. Prioritizing Self-Care: May acknowledges the significance of self-care and deliberately chooses to prioritize her well-being. She takes active steps to nurture her physical, emotional, and mental health. Whether it's engaging in activities she enjoys, practicing mindfulness, seeking therapy, or taking breaks when needed, her choices reflect her commitment to self-care and contribute to her overall well-being.

6. Nurturing Supportive Relationships: May recognizes that the choices she makes regarding her relationships impact her emotional well-being. She consciously chooses to surround herself with people who support and uplift her. May fosters connections with individuals who share her values and encourage her personal growth. These choices in relationships contribute to her emotional resilience and reinforce her self-assurance.

7. Embracing Positivity and Gratitude: May actively chooses to embrace positivity and gratitude in her daily life. She cultivates a habit of focusing on the good things, practicing gratitude, and choosing positive thoughts and perspectives. These choices help shift her mindset towards optimism, enhancing her emotional well-being and boosting her self-assurance.

By making intentional choices that align with her core values, practicing self-care, nurturing supportive relationships, and adopting a growth mindset, May prioritizes her emotional and mental well-being. These choices empower her to rewrite her narrative, regain self-assurance, and create a fulfilling and thriving life.

CHAPTER 10:

PERIODIC REFLECTION: THE SIGNIFICANCE OF REVIEWING YOUR JOURNEY.

Our individual journeys are intricate threads woven together by our experiences, choices, and lessons learned. We embark on our paths with hopes, dreams, and aspirations, often navigating uncharted territories as we seek personal and professional growth. However, in the hustle and bustle of daily life, it's easy to lose sight of where we started and where we are headed. This chapter invites you to take a pause, a moment of introspection, and consider the profound significance of periodic reflection on your journey.

The Unexamined Life

"The unexamined life is not worth living," declared the ancient Greek philosopher, Socrates. His words resonate through the ages, reminding us that without introspection, life loses much of its meaning and purpose. Periodic reflection is the act of intentionally pausing to contemplate our past, present, and future. It's a practice that allows us to connect the dots in our lives, identify patterns, acknowledge our accomplishments, and learn from our failures.

Consider a ship navigating the vast ocean. Without periodic checks on its course, it may drift aimlessly, veering off track. Similarly, without periodic reflection, we risk drifting away from our goals, values, and aspirations. It's easy to become so engrossed in the day-to-day activities that we lose sight of our larger vision. However, taking time for introspection can help us stay on course and ensure that our actions align with our truest selves.

Celebrating Milestones

Periodic reflection isn't just about identifying areas for improvement; it's also about celebrating milestones and achievements. Think of it as a moment to pat yourself on the back for the progress you've made. Life is filled with small victories, and when we take time to acknowledge them, we cultivate gratitude and boost our motivation.

Imagine a mountain climber scaling a steep peak. Along the way, there are ledges where they can catch their breath, appreciate the breathtaking views, and revel in the satisfaction of reaching new heights. These moments of reflection serve as motivators, encouraging them to continue their ascent. Similarly, reflecting on your journey's milestones can serve as stepping stones toward your greater objectives.

Learning from Setbacks

Life is not a continuous upward trajectory. It's a series of peaks and valleys, highs and lows. Periodic reflection helps us embrace these inevitable setbacks as opportunities for growth. Instead of viewing failures as roadblocks, we can see them as stepping stones toward success.

Consider a scientist in a laboratory. When an experiment fails, they don't abandon their pursuit; they analyse what went wrong, make adjustments, and try again. In a similar vein, periodic reflection allows us to examine our failures, learn from them, and course correct. It's a chance to ask ourselves, "What can I do differently next time?" This growth mindset empowers us to persevere and continue our journey with resilience.

Aligning with Your Values

As we evolve, our values and priorities may shift. Periodic reflection helps us ensure that our actions align with our current values. Sometimes, we pursue goals that were once important but have lost their relevance. By reflecting on our values, we can realign our path with what truly matters to us.

Imagine a compass guiding a hiker through a dense forest. If the hiker doesn't occasionally check the compass, they might veer off course, unaware that they're no longer headed in the right direction. Similarly, periodic reflection acts as our moral compass, guiding us toward our true north.

Crafting Your Next Steps

Ultimately, periodic reflection isn't solely about looking back; it's also about looking forward. It's an opportunity to craft a roadmap for your future, set new goals, and dream bigger dreams. By assessing where you are now and where you want to go, you can create actionable plans to bridge the gap.

Picture an architect designing a blueprint for a magnificent skyscraper. They start with a vision, but the blueprint is the detailed plan that brings that vision to life. Similarly, periodic reflection helps you create your life's blueprint, outlining the steps needed to build the future you desire.

In the frenetic pace of modern life, it's easy to lose sight of our personal journeys amidst the noise and distractions. However, by embracing the practice of periodic reflection, we can regain clarity, celebrate our achievements, learn from our setbacks, align with our values, and craft a brighter future.

Periodic reflection is not a luxury; it's a necessity on the journey of self-discovery and personal growth. So, take a moment to pause, breathe, and contemplate your path. It's through these reflective moments that you can truly begin again, armed with a deeper understanding of yourself and the direction you want to take in life.

The Art of Reflection

Reflection is a practice as old as humanity itself. From ancient philosophers to modern thinkers, individuals have recognized the profound impact of contemplation on personal growth and development. Periodic reflection involves intentionally setting aside time to review your life's journey, taking stock of your experiences, and gaining insight into your personal evolution.

In our fast-paced world, where the days blend into one another, the art of reflection has become increasingly scarce. We often prioritize productivity and busyness over mindfulness and self-awareness. However, to "Begin Again," we must pause and acknowledge where we've been before charting our course forward.

Why Reflect?

Periodic reflection provides us with a bird's-eye view of our lives. It helps us see patterns, recognize recurring themes, and identify the areas where we've grown or remained stagnant.

By reflecting on your journey, you become more attuned to your values, beliefs, strengths, and weaknesses. This self-awareness empowers you to make informed decisions and live in alignment with your true self.

Celebrate Achievements, Life's journey is filled with accomplishments, both big and small. Reflecting on your successes reminds you of your resilience and capabilities, boosting your confidence and motivation.

Adversity is a great teacher. Reflecting on the challenges you've faced allows you to extract valuable lessons, fostering resilience and adaptability.

Periodic reflection helps you refine your goals and aspirations. It allows you to assess whether your current path aligns with your long-term objectives, making it easier to adjust your course if necessary.

By reflecting on your interactions and experiences with others, you can identify areas for improvement in your relationships. This can lead to more meaningful connections and deeper empathy.

How to Reflect?

Find a peaceful and distraction-free environment where you can think without interruptions.

Schedule regular periods for reflection. It could be daily, weekly, or monthly, depending on your preferences and availability.

Journaling: Writing down your thoughts and feelings is a powerful way to facilitate reflection. Use a journal to record your experiences, emotions, and insights.

Meditation can help you quiet your mind and gain clarity. Engage in mindfulness practices to stay present and focused during your reflection.

Challenge yourself with thought-provoking questions, such as: "What have I learned recently?" "What am I grateful for?" and "What can I improve?"

Revisit your goals and aspirations regularly. Are they still relevant? Are you making progress towards them?

Reach out to trusted friends, mentors, or family members for their perspectives on your journey. Their insights can provide valuable external viewpoints.

CONCLUSION

In "Begin Again," we've embarked on a journey of self-discovery, growth, and transformation.

As you continue reading through the chapters of your life, remember to pause, take a step back, and reflect. In these moments of introspection, you'll find the clarity and wisdom to "Begin Again" with renewed purpose and determination. Periodic reflection is not just a chapter; it's an ongoing narrative that guides us towards our truest selves and our most fulfilling lives.

Remember that rewriting your story is a process that requires patience, dedication, and perseverance. It's important to take it one step at a time and be kind to yourself along the way. With effort and commitment, you can create a new narrative for your life that reflects the person you want to be that aligns with your values and aspirations. It's also important to acknowledge that change is not always easy, and there may be obstacles and setbacks along the way. However, by staying focused on your goals, seeking support from others, and learning from your experiences, you can overcome these challenges and continue to make progress towards the life you want to create. Remember to celebrate your successes no matter how small they may seem, and to stay motivated and persistent in pursuing your dreams.

ACKNOWLEDGEMENTS

I would like to thank everyone who assisted me in planning and reviewing the manuscript. May the Lord richly bless you. To all my family and friends, thank you for the time you took to listen and for your love and patience. I am grateful for all your contributions and support throughout my life and this project. I am grateful to the community, who have been there for me in one way or the other throughout my life. Thank you to my pastors and leaders. I have sat under their leadership over the years. May you continue to share the transforming message of Christ's love for us.

Special thanks to my husband, Tawanda and my two boys, Joel, and Rodnie-Jude for all the love, sacrifice, and support. I love you.

May the Lord richly bless you.

Contact details are as follows.

lynn@nurtureandequip.com

Facebook - Lynn Chitsatso

Instagram - Lynn chitsatso

Elmlink.co/beginagainthebook

REFERENCES

Peter Drucker, The Practice of Management, Management by Objectives (MBO)

Aligning Objectives With Organizational Goals By the Mind Tools Content Team

Beyond Performance 2.0: A Proven Approach to Leading Large-Scale Change (John Wiley & Sons, July 2019 https://www.mckinsey.com/capabilities/people-and-organizational-performance/our-insights/getting-personal-about-change

KL Bailey 2021 The Effect of Cognitive Behaviour Therapy on Improving Academic Performance of Depressed Young Adults

Rupčić, N. (2017), "Spiritual development – a missing and powerful leverage when building learning organizations", The Learning Organization,

- Scripture quotations are from the ESV® Bible (The Holy Bible, English Standard Version®), copyright © 2001 by Crossway, a publishing ministry of Good News Publishers. Used by permission. All rights reserved."

- Scripture quotations marked (NIV) are taken from the Holy Bible, New International Version®, NIV®. Copyright © 1973, 1978, 1984, 2011 by Biblica, Inc.™ Used by permission of Zondervan. All rights reserved worldwide. www.zondervan.com The "NIV" and "New International Version" are trademarks registered in the United States Patent and Trademark Office by Biblica, Inc.™

- ERV - "Taken from the Holy Bible: Easy-To-Read Version © 2001 by World Bible Translation Centre, Inc. and used by permission. Scriptures marked KJV are taken from the KING JAMES VERSION (KJV): KING JAMES VERSION, public domain.

Printed in Great Britain
by Amazon

38359353R00089